HOW TO TEACH ABROAD

In this Series

other titles in preparation

How To Books: General Editor Roland Seymour

TEACH ABROAD

Roger Jones

Northcote House

© Copyright 1989 by Roger Jones

First published in 1989 by Northcote House Publishers Ltd,
Harper & Row House, Estover Road, Plymouth PL6 7PZ,
United Kingdom. Tel: Plymouth (0752) 705251. Telex: 45635.
Fax: (0752) 777603.

British Library Cataloguing in Publication Data

Jones, Roger, *1942-*
  How to teach abroad. — (How to books)
  1. Teaching — Career guides
  I. Title
  371.1′02′023

  ISBN 0-7463-0551-6

Typeset by Cheshire Typesetters
Printed and bound in Great Britain by BPCC Wheatons Ltd, Exeter

Contents

Preface

One of the characteristics of the second half of the twentieth century has been the expansion in education in virtually every country in the world. In the developed world the increase in provision has perhaps been less noticeable than in Third World countries where education was once the privilege of an élite, and where strenuous efforts are now underway to achieve universal education for their populations.

However, many countries fall short of their goal simply because they lack teachers and lecturers capable of providing the quality of education they need. So they have to call on an international pool of educationists who are ready and willing to leave home and offer their expertise in different lands.

Teachers from the British Isles form a significant proportion of this international pool. They have the advantage of speaking the international language of education — English — and have the reputation for being adaptable. However, that does not mean their experience abroad is always trouble-free. Problems occur, and it is as well to consider potential hazards before leaving these shores.

One of the purposes of this book is to make people aware of the trials and benefits of teaching overseas. It won't answer every question nor deal with every problem you are likely to encounter. The world is a vast place and no two countries are the same. What the book does do is put forward the pros and cons of teaching abroad, to enable you to decide whether it is a sensible option or not, and — for those who are stouthearted enough to wish to continue — offer a few facts which will enable you to choose a direction, and provide signposts to further sources of information. The book also highlights matters you ought to go into and questions you need to ask before you come to a decision.

At times it may seem to some readers that I am stating the obvious. Please bear with me — what is obvious to a veteran of several overseas summers may not be so for a person taking up his or her first teaching post abroad.

I am indebted to a number of people without whose help this undertaking would have been impossible. They include teacher recruitment organisations, members of virtually every diplomatic mission based in London, officials of a number of foreign ministries of education, Dorothy Garland of the Association of Commonwealth Universities, David Harper and Clementine Alfonso of the British Council, Claire Shoesmith of Christians Abroad, Helen Roseblade of CMS, Dr Terence Gerighty of ELT Banbury, Deborah Jordan of ECIS, Ken Cripwell of the London University Institute of Education, John Haycraft and Cathy Connolly of International House, John Cleaver of International Language Centres, Patricia Swain of the League for the Exchange of Commonwealth Teachers, Beryl Hulbert of the Methodist Church Overseas Division, John Rowe of NUT, Fiona Leach of OCTAB, Gerald Owen, Christopher Pearson, Kate Pearce, Desmond Thomas, J.L. Backhouse, Katy Smith, Alistair Walker, Robert Butterfield and many others.

Finally, a warning. I have not had the opportunity personally to inspect all the countries, schools and educational systems mentioned in the book. Life, alas, is too short. But I have sought wherever possible the best informed opinion. Furthermore, information of the sort included in this book quickly goes out of date. Please treat the book as a guide, and not as the last word in accuracy.

To all of you who are teaching abroad or are planning to do so I offer my best wishes for the success of your venture.

Roger Jones

1
Doors of Opportunity

THE ATTRACTIONS OF TEACHING ABROAD

Judging from the millions of people who take their holidays abroad each year foreign climes have their attractions. Sometimes it is the warmer climate which entices people away from their native shores; sometimes it is the scenery, or the cultural treasures, or the atmosphere of the place.

Some people become so enamoured with the place that they look into the possibility of staying there for an extended period of time. Unless you have a private income, such a plan usually entails looking round for a job. Teachers and lecturers are particularly well placed when it comes to finding employment, although the availability of jobs tends to vary according to your subject.

There are other attractions, too. There is the opportunity to gain valuable experience, and a certain amount of overseas work on your CV might well impress discerning selectors at some future date. There is also the opportunity — in certain countries — to earn a substantial salary which could have the added attraction of being tax-free.

THE RANGE OF OPPORTUNITIES

Short-term

How short-term is short-term? It could be a matter of just a month or two on a vacation course. Or it could be half a year. Sometimes schools and colleges need to replace staff who have left or fallen ill, and are ready to employ someone on a short-term basis.

At the senior level there may be an opportunity to do short consultancies — perhaps on secondment from your employer.

One year

A number of organisations offer one year renewable contracts. There may be a number of reasons for this. The place may be somewhat un-congenial so that employers doubt whether they will attract people on a long-term basis or there may be legal reasons, as would be the case if you have to obtain a work permit every year.

Two to three years
Many of the contracts tend to be two or three year ones, especially public sector appointments. In many cases such contracts are renewable.

A long-term career
For anyone thinking in terms of teaching abroad as a long-term com-mitment, there is a snag. It is comparatively rare to find a post offer-ing security of tenure. Virtually all posts are contract posts of up to a maximum of three years. You live from one contract to another, and can miss out on perks such as in-service training and pension schemes.

There are several reasons for this. First, in the Third World especially, you are really filling in until a suitable local person can take over your position. Secondly, political upheavals can occur which may render it impossible for you to continue with your work, as has happened in Lebanon. Thirdly, your employability rating may decline if you stay in one place too long (see Chapter 6).

WEIGHING UP THE PROS AND CONS

Before you embark on a contract of a year or more, consider the social and professional implications at the outset. A lot will depend on the stage you have reached in your teaching career, but for the sake of con-venience I have divided people into three categories:

- **young teachers:** teachers in their twenties who are at the beginning of their careers
- **mid-term teachers:** teachers in their thirties and early forties who may well have family commitments
- **mature teachers:** teachers in their mid-forties onwards.

As a *young teacher* you need to get plenty of experience, and so it doesn't make sense to stay too long at a particular post. If you are plan-ning to settle down to a career in the UK it is advisable not to stay abroad too long, or you may find it more difficult to land a post commen-surate with your experience when you eventually return.

Mid-term teachers with families are often in a dilemma when their offspring reach secondary level, particularly if there are no suitable schools locally for them. Professionally this is a time when decisions have to be made which will affect your long-term future. If you opt for overseas service, is there chance you'll miss a promotion at home?

If you stay overseas too long, will you be able to get back into the system?

As a *mature teacher* you probably know how you want your career to develop and may no longer be encumbered with youthful dependants. You are able to please yourself and may think of teaching overseas as a second career offering challenges you are unlikely to get at home.

ARE YOU THE TYPE?

What qualities and qualifications are required in anyone venturing abroad?

- adaptability
- open-mindedness
- stability
- good health
- tact

- curiosity
- patience
- resourcefulness
- a sense of humour
- good qualifications

Adaptability

This is obviously the first thing that springs to mind. The kind of person who expects life to be exactly the same as back home is in for a shock. A capacity to adapt may be required on a number of fronts, the most crucial being:

- professional adaptability. You could find that syllabuses and teaching methods are strictly regulated by the government. Or you may find that you are constrained by poor textbooks and enormous classes.

- environmental adaptability. You could find yourself in a place where you are surrounded by abject poverty, or where the differences between rich and poor are very much pronounced. You may find that your social life is restricted to a very small, inward-looking community.
- cultural adaptability. There are national differences in temperament, outlook and behaviour to be aware of and to accept. For instance, it is quite customary for men to kiss each other in parts of Southern Europe and the Arab World, while in parts of Asia such physical demonstrations of affection tend to be avoided — even between the sexes.

Open-mindedness

Although there is more than one way of solving a problem, expatriates are sometimes bewildered by the way other nationals set about their tasks. Yet foreign methods may be just as valid as your own, and you need to be prepared to accept them and even adopt them.

Stability

If you are prone to nervous breakdowns or have problems in coming to terms with life, a foreign posting will rarely provide the relatively sheltered environment which you may think you need to exist. Indeed, people living abroad are frequently exposed to much greater stresses and strains than at home, so if you believe that a spell abroad will help you through a bad patch — forget it!

Good health

Certain climates can prove trying for people who are not in the best of health. Some people find it difficult to withstand excessive heat or high altitudes; nasty infections can lay you low, particularly in tropical areas. However, if you are reasonably healthy and take sensible precautions, you have very little to worry about.

Tact

In a sense every expatriate is a representative of his or her country, and this means you need to act diplomatically. If you are adept at the ready retort, you may find this does not go down particularly well with the locals. They may misunderstand, and equate your down-to-earth bluntness with rudeness.

Curiosity

Your natural curiosity could stand you in good stead, provided you don't take it to extremes — to understand a country and its people, and make the most of the experience, you need to be keen to find out all you can about the place.

Patience

You may have to deal with inefficient bureaucracies; you may find that your students are less alert and slower to learn than you have been led to believe. If you are impatient to succeed at the job, the chances are that you won't!

Resourcefulness

There will probably be occasions where you have to rely on yourself to solve problems, particularly if you are in a fairly isolated spot. This could range from making teaching aids out of nothing to repairing the plumbing.

A sense of humour

Many agencies I talked to mentioned this as a desirable quality. Unless you are able to laugh at yourself and the situations in which you find yourself from time to time, you could find life quite unbearable.

Good qualifications

Good qualifications are also important. Most countries hold qualified people in high regard. The more experience you have and the more impressive your qualifications, the higher your status will be within the academic community. Indeed, you will not get a job abroad unless your qualifications are adequate. This applies to volunteer posts as much as to fully-paid contract posts.

However, exceptionally well-qualified people are not necessarily the most successful in a foreign environment. There have been instances of overseas institutions recruiting PhDs for quite low level teaching. If you are an intellectual powerhouse you may become frustrated if there are few, if any, facilities for pursuing your research.

WHERE CAN I TEACH?

It is tempting to believe that the world is your oyster, but in fact it never is. Even so, there are British teachers in virtually every country of the world teaching all manner of subjects.

If your particular specialisation is very much in demand, like Teaching English as a Foreign Language (TEFL), then you have a wide choice, though this will probably exclude English-speaking countries. There is also a high demand for science and maths specialists. If your speciality is in the arts or social sciences, there are fewer openings. However, occasional posts do arise, in Commonwealth universities for example, and in Commonwealth countries on teacher exchanges. There are also schools in foreign localities which cater largely for expatriates.

If you are prepared to venture outside your specialism — into TEFL, for instance — the range of opportunities will widen. Some TEFL employers will accept people on the strength of their teacher's certificate and proven ability to teach.

THE REWARDS

The teaching profession in Britain has not produced many millionaires and this also holds true for the teaching fraternity in other countries, despite reports of astronomical tax-free salaries in the oil-rich countries of the Middle East.

When you look at salaries offered you need to see what the total package entails. It could include free accommodation, free medical insurance, and free education for your children. On the other hand, there may be no accommodation element at all, and this could make the salary less attractive than it seems.

At the other end of the scale come the volunteer and missionary posts. These are for people for whom income is not an important consideration. Their attraction lies in the type of experience they offer and the opportunity to serve one's fellow men. You will have enough to live on, certainly, but not enough to service whatever financial commitments you have at home.

Other rewards are less tangible. You have an opportunity to travel, to extend your circle of friends, to become acquainted with different cultures, to enjoy pleasanter climates (perhaps), and experience a different lifestyle. Much will depend on what benefits you are looking for.

One warning: you must dispel any idea that working abroad is one long holiday. Indeed, it involves at least the same responsibilities, frustrations, pressures and sense of commitment that you would experience in your work at home. In one sense it can be disarmingly different; in another it is more of the same.

WHAT TYPE OF INSTITUTION?

So far we have been considering the option of teaching abroad in very general terms. Of course, no-one teaches in a vacuum, and your experiences will be shaped by the type of institution to which you are attached. The range of teaching institutions which recruit expatriates is extremely varied. Some will be similar to schools and colleges which you have worked in at home. Others will be very strange and unfamiliar — both in their appearance and their practices. This section attempts to classify them.

PRIMARY AND SECONDARY SECTOR

There are two distinctly different types of school or college in this sector:

● those which cater for children from the expatriate community (**expatriate schools**), some of which open their doors to local children, and
● those which cater solely for the nationals of the country in question (**indigenous schools**).

Expatriate schools

Most of these schools will be organised along familiar lines. The pattern will usually be British or American, and your colleagues will be largely expatriate. The teachers will be birds of passage on two- or three-year contracts like yourself, though you may find some old hands, notably wives who are married to nationals.

Vacancies occur for teachers of most subjects.

Service schools

These schools are exclusively for the children of army, navy or air force personnel and are usually on base. They are financed by the Ministry of Defence and are run along exactly the same lines as a school in Britain. Such schools exist in Belgium, Brunei, Cyprus, Denmark, West Germany, Gibraltar, Hong Kong, Italy, Nepal, Norway and Sardinia. The majority cater for the primary age range.

International schools

These schools provide an education for children from the expatriate community, and in many cases local children also attend. The curriculum of English medium schools usually follows the British or American pattern.

Some are private ventures, others may have official backing, while others are run by a foundation. In certain countries they are limited to the children of embassy staff and other expatriates in official positions; in others over 50% of the clientele could be locals.

Among the most prestigious of these schools are those run by United World Colleges (of which Atlantic College is one). The European Community Schools are also highly regarded — there is one such school at Culham in Oxfordshire which caters, like the others, for the children of EC officials and offers the type of education children would receive in their respective countries.

There are also schools which serve the expatriate communities of other countries — French and German schools, for example. Generally speaking such schools employ teachers trained in France or Germany and provide a French or German style education. In the Middle East there are a number of bilingual Arabic/English schools primarily for the expatriate Arab community.

Other opportunities
Vacancies occasionally occur for private tutors — usually for the children of very rich and aristocratic families.

Indigenous schools

Teaching in a school catering for the nationals of your adoptive country is likely to contrast strikingly with your experience in the UK.

- You may find you are the only British person on the staff.
- The operation of the school may be quite different from what you are used to.
- The pupils you have to deal with may respond differently to your teaching methods. Pupils in the Far East, for example, may seem unduly passive, while those in some Middle Eastern countries, though eager, may lack self-control.

Any teacher planning to work in such a school will need to be **adaptable.** Don't assume you will be able to teach and behave just as you did back home, and make sure you know in advance what will be expected of you. In schools where expatriates are thin on the ground you may be regarded as something of a novelty.

Teachers of English are in great demand in non-English-speaking countries. In Western European countries this need is catered for principally by exchange assistantships operated by the Central Bureau for Educational Visits and Exchanges. Certain Governments (Hong Kong, Singapore and Malaysia) have recruited substantial numbers of English teachers on a short-term basis in a bid to improve standards.

There are opportunities for teachers of other subjects in English- and non-English-speaking countries. However, they are not usually required (except on an exchange basis) where there is a sufficient pool of indigenous teachers. In certain Third World countries there is a shortage of qualified teachers in most subjects, but since such countries are usually short of cash, many of the openings for teachers are on volunteer or missionary terms.

State schools

The majority of openings for teachers are in the secondary sector — or intermediate and secondary sector, where this distinction exists. There is a considerable variation in standards between countries and regions within countries, even within Western Europe.

Some schools will be highly selective, particularly in certain developing countries where secondary education is by no means universal. Some will be progressive in their teaching methods and have plenty of equipment. At the other end of the spectrum, a good many state schools can be grim places housed in inadequate buildings and with few, if any, resources. Generally speaking, the poorer the country, the poorer the facilities.

In the attempt to provide universal education, quality tends to suffer, and schools are starved of cash. In such situations teachers are poorly motivated and poorly paid. Many of them 'moonlight', and have little time or inclination to develop themselves professionally. Not all are properly qualified.

Private schools

Private schools flourish in most countries. In some cases they are felt to offer a superior education to schools in the state sector. In others they have been set up to cope with a demand for education that the state itself is unable to satisfy. Quite a number are English medium.

There are three main types:

- **Church or Mission schools.** These are often well established schools with a good academic reputation. They tend to be fee-paying, but many offer scholarships. In former British possessions many such schools are state aided, and may offer free schooling.
- **Schools run by a foundation.** These schools are usually insulated

from commercial pressures, but even so most tend to be fee-paying. They usually take in a certain proportion of scholarship pupils.

- **Private ventures.** These schools tend to be the most variable of all. Some are very good, while others, particularly in places where the government does not exert strict controls, can be mediocre.

In some countries private schools operate quite independently of the state, and may therefore differ quite markedly from schools in the state sector. This is the case in Greece, for example, where there are British-type schools, American-type schools, etc.

Elsewhere, in neighbouring Turkey for instance, the situation is quite different. All schools are expected to adhere to a centrally controlled curriculum, which means that books, teachers, school buildings and courses have to be approved and inspected by the Ministry of Education.

TERTIARY SECTOR

This sector embraces universities, colleges of education, technical institutes and the like.

Many establishments have openings for English teachers (see Chapter 2), and several — particularly in the Commonwealth — have opportunities in other fields as well, usually on a contract basis. If you are working in a higher education establishment in the UK, you may well have a link with an overseas institution of learning, and may have the chance of being seconded to a teaching post there.

There are also opportunities in international and regional institutes, such as those operated by the South East Asian Ministers of Education Organisation. At this level much of the teaching is done through the medium of English.

It is difficult to generalise about higher education, since every university or polytechnic is likely to be different. Some of the more venerable institutions are still very traditional in their approach, with syllabuses which seem to hark back to the beginning of the century. Others turn out to be very forward-looking.

MISCELLANEOUS

This category covers educational activities which fall outside the formal system of education.

Adult institutes
These offer part-time courses, usually in the evening, for people who wish to extend their knowledge either for professional reasons or as a leisure activity. They are particularly well developed in Scandinavia

and German-speaking countries. The main requirement is for teachers of English.

Language schools
The demand for English seems to be insatiable these days, and in virtually every country there are institutes which offer English tuition on a part-time or a full-time basis. The clientele tends to be adult, with a preponderance of students in their late teens and early twenties. Some take younger age groups, particularly in countries where the quality of language tuition in schools is poor.

The British Council, like other cultural institutes, is involved with language courses in many countries, either through its own direct teaching operations (DTEOs) or in collaboration with a local foundation. However, many language schools are private ventures, some affiliated to organisations in the UK or US (such as International House) or are branches of large language training companies (such as Berlitz). Native English speakers are much in demand as teachers in these institutes.

In-house training programmes
In-house training is a growing field, and many large companies and government organisations have their own in-house facilities for updating and developing the expertise of their staff. In most cases the lecturers will be nationals of the country in question, but this is not always true in the developing world and on language training programmes.

Companies operating overseas are often required to provide a training package in addition to supplying equipment. British Aerospace, for instance, not only provides Saudi Arabia with jets, but it also trains pilots and ground staff in such fields as navigation, maintenance and English. Oil, health care and engineering companies are among the others that operate training programmes.

Vacation courses
There are short term opportunities mainly for English (TEFL) teachers and sports teachers at summer camps and holiday resorts for young people. For further details consult *Working Holidays* published by the Central Bureau for Educational Visits and Exchanges.

2
Subjects to Teach Abroad

THE TEFL CHALLENGE

One of your greatest assets is your mother-tongue — English. English is the international *lingua franca* par excellence, and anyone involved in international commerce, politics and travel who does not possess at least a rudimentary knowledge of the language is at a tremendous disadvantage professionally.

The upshot of this is that people are eager to learn English, and there is a huge demand for teachers of the subject. In some places people are so desperate to learn that they will turn to any English speaker for help, whether that person is a trained teacher or not. People like this have probably picked up the rudiments of English at school, but they lack practice, particularly in speaking English. A person has much more chance to practice oral skills in an informal one-to-one situation — whether the informant is a qualified teacher or not — than in the more formal atmosphere of a classroom containing perhaps thirty, forty or fifty pupils.

THE QUALIFICATIONS REQUIRED

These will vary considerably. For the assistantship scheme of the Central Bureau for Educational Visits and Exchanges no prior experience of TEFL is usually demanded, but teachers may be expected to follow an induction course before setting off. Some language schools are prepared to take on people with no experience, but placement may be dependent on the candidate completing one of their own training programmes.

Generally, the minimum qualification for a TEFL teaching post is now the RSA Preparatory Certificate in Teaching English as a Foreign Language to Adults (TEFLA). Employers, however, tend to prefer teachers with some experience of teaching abroad. This is particularly important in the case of posts involving an element of responsibility.

In such cases evidence of more rigorous training will be expected, such as the RSA Diploma in Teaching English as a Foreign Language to Adults or a Postgraduate Certificate of Education (PGCE) in TEFL. A higher degree (eg an MA in Applied Linguistics) is now becoming essential for more senior posts.

TEFL training

A generation ago there were only a handful of courses to prepare teachers for teaching English to foreigners. Now there are courses in all shapes and sizes.

Full-time courses.
- One year courses leading to a postgraduate certificate in education, many of which are recognised by the Department of Education and Science.
- Advanced courses for experienced teachers leading to a Diploma or Master's Degree.
- BEd courses which include a TEFL component.

Part-time courses. Many of these lead to the RSA TEFLA Diploma or Preparatory Certificate. International House has a distance learning programme leading to the former which runs from July to May.

Short intensive courses. These may be organised by large language institutes and are intended primarily for teachers taking up vacancies in their schools (eg Inlingua) or as induction courses for assistants and volunteers. International House runs a four-week introductory course leading to the RSA Certificate and Diploma.

There is a list of courses and addresses on pages 26 and 27.

THE RANGE OF TEFL POSTS ABROAD

Secondary level
State schools
Most of the assistantships handled by the Central Bureau are in government schools. In the developing world many of the teaching posts in government schools are for volunteers.

Opportunities exist for experienced teachers in countries which do not have enough English teachers of their own or are anxious to raise standards. This is particularly the case at present in parts of the Middle East and South East Asia, notably in relatively prosperous countries.

Private secondary schools
Well established English medium schools with a substantial expatriate clientele will probably have no need for TEFL teachers at all.

Others will, and they range from missionary schools, schools belonging to foundations, and private enterprise establishments. Middle class parents in many countries believe that a thorough grounding in English is the passport to a good job, and the presence of a native English speaker on the staff of a school often acts as a considerable incentive for them to enrol their children there.

Tertiary level

English has become a medium of instruction for many subjects at university now, and a large proportion of undergraduates and most postgraduates will need to read and consult textbooks written in English.

As a consequence there are three types of English teaching activities:

- **Traditional courses** in English departments including literature, composition, linguistics, English life and institutions for students studying for an English degree.
- **Teacher training courses** designed to turn out people who are able to teach effectively in secondary schools and sometimes at university level.
- **Service English courses** for students of other subjects for whom English is the key to the proper understanding of their chosen subject, eg science, economics, engineering. Service courses may be run concurrently with the study programme, or be intensive programmes which take place before the study programme begins. Often acceptance on the study programme is dependent on a student acquiring proficiency in English.

Government language institutes

In several countries there are language institutes for training civil servants or the military, sometimes independent, sometimes attached to ministries, such as the Foreign Ministry or Ministry of Defence, and sometimes attached to universities. Possible clientele will be diplomats, officials going on courses abroad, or officials who need to deal with foreigners in the course of their work.

Large international organisations, such as the UN in New York, also have language training programmes for their staff.

Private language institutes

These are usually commercial organisations which take all comers. The age range can be considerable, but tending towards students in their teens and twenties. Many prepare their students either for national examinations or international tests such as Cambridge Proficiency and Lower Certificate. Some may provide in-company language training outside the institute.

While most tend to be independent organisations, others may be members of a national chain (eg the British School in Italy). Alternatively they may be part of, or affiliated to, an international group (Inlingua, International House, ELT).

Courses can vary considerably, even within one school — some may be full-time and intensive, with anything from one to 25 students per class, but the majority will probably be part-time, for those who come along in their spare time. As a consequence many schools operate in the evening and even at weekends in some countries. The 9 to 5 day is the exception rather than the rule in this sector.

The quality of the premises and the teaching can also vary. Some organisations pay badly and as a consequence lack properly qualified teachers.

On the whole, private language schools are for the single and unencumbered, though some organisations are able to accommodate teaching couples. Senior positions in these organisations offer better salaries and sometimes a few perks.

Cultural Associations

Other language schools are operated by cultural organisations such as the British Council, which has 51 direct teaching operations (DTEOs) in some 45 countries.

Elsewhere, there are non-profitmaking cultural associations, such as the Turco-British Association, which run similar operations. These generally have a link with the local British Council office and may well be housed in the same building.

Courses like these are generally highly regarded locally, and the staff are likely to be a mix of locally recruited teachers and those recruited from England and elsewhere.

Companies

Large companies may well have language training programmes for their staff, with both full-time and part-time vacancies. Companies with large contracts overseas often have to provide a training package for local staff which contains a substantial EFL component.

Private tuition

This is another option. Teachers often take on private students to supplement their earnings at a language institute. It is possible, once you have established a reputation for yourself in a locality, to concentrate entirely on private students. Care must be taken, however, that you do not fall foul of the residence laws.

Miscellaneous

For experienced TEFL practitioners there are advisory posts, generally within ministries of education but sometimes attached to tertiary institutions. Other opportunities may occur within the educational inspectorate and educational broadcasting.

PROSPECTS FOR TEFL TEACHERS RETURNING TO THE UK

One problem that returnees come up against is that the majority of posts in TEFL are seasonal.

Language schools

There are language schools dotted all over Britain offering courses for foreigners, most of them private. Many of them are open all through the year, but business tends to be slack during the autumn and winter, so you may only be offered a short-term contract at first.

Local education authorities

LEAs with a substantial immigrant community often have special units within schools to improve the language of non-natives. Many of these jobs are full-time and offer the same terms and conditions as those enjoyed by other teachers employed by the authority.

Colleges, polytechnics and universities

If you have substantial experience you might consider going into teacher training. Some organisations also run English courses for foreign students all the year round but opportunities tend to be restricted and competition is keen.

Department of Employment Training Agency

Among the Government's training schemes is one designed to upgrade the language skills of immigrant workers. More details are available in the booklet *Action for Jobs* or from Job Centres.

Permanent openings

If you plan to settle in the British Isles, it may be necessary to consider a change of career direction. Here are a few suggestions:

- Modern language teaching. Good language teachers are currently in short supply.
- Publishing. Publishers involved in the lucrative EFL textbook market are often on the lookout for editors and writers.
- Working with foreign firms or missions. Opportunities arise in UK based diplomatic and commercial missions, foreign banks and companies. Your knowledge of a particular country could compensate for your lack of experience in this area.

POTENTIAL PITFALLS FOR A TEFL TEACHER

Linguistic chauvinism

Enthusiastic but inexperienced English teachers often see their subject as the most important on the curriculum but it never is (except in the case of language schools). If you come in that category you may be somewhat chastened to find that your students, particularly the younger ones, do not show much enthusiasm for your native tongue, and seem to be irritatingly slow at picking it up. Bear in mind that language learning is a chore which does not yield immediate returns. As a language specialist you should make an effort to come to grips with the mother tongue of your students — often a very sobering exercise.

'I'm the expert' attitude

Your English may be more fluent than that of your native-born colleagues, but it does not follow that you are a more capable teacher than they are. After all, most of them have had to learn English from scratch and are consequently more aware of the problems their pupils face.

Don't be patronising. They will resent you for it. Don't presume to teach them how to teach, unless you are employed as a teacher trainer. And don't push the type of methodology which you used with great success at a summer school at home, since it could prove to be completely inappropriate.

Inflexibility

The most successful TEFL teachers tend to be those who can adapt to local circumstances and expectations. No matter how keen you are about a certain method of teaching or a particular textbook, you may have to accept that it doesn't work with your students.

This is particularly true in primary and secondary schools. Indeed, some of the most successful teachers of TEFL at this level turn out to be those with several years' experience in schools back home specialising in subjects other than TEFL, and with no axes to grind.

COURSES PROVIDING TRAINING IN TEFL

RSA Diploma in Teaching English as a Foreign Language to Adults

Details available from Royal Society of Arts, Murray Road, Orpington, Kent BR5 3RB.

Courses in Altrincham, Bedford, Birmingham (Polytechnic), Bournemouth, Bristol (Brunel), Broadstairs, Cambridge, Cheltenham, Chichester, Chippenham, Colchester, Eastbourne, Edinburgh, Hastings, Pinner, Hove, Kettering, Leicester, Liverpool, London — Ealing, Hammersmith, Waltham Forest, Luton, Manchester (Central), Northwich, Norwich (Bell), Nottingham, Oxford, Saffron Walden, Stoke-on-Trent, Southampton, Southend, Torquay.

Trinity College Licentiate Diploma in the Teaching of English as a Foreign or Second Language

Details available from Trinity College, 11-13 Mandeville Place, London W1M 6AQ.

Courses are held in Aberdeen, Cheltenham, Colchester, Esher, Godalming, Cleveland, Tetford (Notts), Sheffield, Twickenham, Woking, Sheffield.

Postgraduate Certificate in Education with TEFL as main or subsidiary subject

Birmingham Polytechnic, Leicester University, London University Institute of Education, Manchester Polytechnic, Manchester University.

Postgraduate Certificate of Education with TEFL as a subsidiary subject

Bognor Regis (West Sussex Institute of Higher Education), Canterbury (Christchurch College), Edinburgh (Moray House College), Twickenham (St Mary's College), Sheffield University, University of Wales — Aberystwyth, Bangor, Cardiff, Warwick University.

Other institutions offering courses in TEFL and allied subjects
Aston University, Birmingham University, Bristol University, Durham University, Edinburgh University, Essex University, Exeter University, Lancaster University, Leeds University, Liverpool University, Polytechnic of Central London, Newcastle University, Nottingham University, Reading University, College of St Mark & St John (Plymouth), Salford University, Stirling University, UWIST, York University.

Further details are provided in two booklets published by the British Council and obtainable from their English Teaching Information Centre, Spring Gardens, London SW1A 2BN:

TEFL/TESL academic courses in the UK — Brief list
TEFL and specialised English courses — Short courses

OPPORTUNITIES IN OTHER SUBJECT AREAS

Although TEFL teachers may appear to have all the advantages, these are inevitably confined to countries outside the English-speaking world. Teachers in other subject areas can have the best of both worlds — they can find a ready market for their skills in any school or university where English is the medium of instruction.

Such institutions are not confined to the British Isles, North America and Australasia. English is also the main language of many Commonwealth countries in Africa, the Caribbean and the Pacific. Moreover it is widely used in tertiary institutions, in the Middle and Far East for example. And finally it is the medium of instruction for many of the international schools to be found in over 150 countries throughout the world.

PRIMARY AND SECONDARY EDUCATION

Service schools
The **Service Children's Education Authority** handles these posts. Service schools require teachers in all subjects, especially primary school teachers in Germany, Cyprus, Hong Kong and Gibraltar. The SCEA recruits some 200 primary teachers annually and 100 secondary teachers. The majority of the latter are required for British military bases in North Germany.

Applicants need to have two years' recent experience in UK schools and be below the age of 47. Salaries are based on the Baker scale plus London weighting and certain allowances which vary according to the size of one's family and the location. You may also have access to duty free goods. The first two tours are of three years each; subsequent ones last five years.

While teaching duties will not differ markedly from those in a school in the UK, there is a far greater turnover of pupils, just as you would find in a school based in a garrison town. Amenities may be poor and some pupils may have adjustment problems. Some schools are boarding establishments which will involve teachers in extra duties.

A teacher's social life will be different, too. You will be mixing a lot with service personnel and their families and must therefore be able to accept the values of military life. Professional commitment and an outgoing personality are important.

International schools

Recruitment for these schools is handled either by the schools themselves through advertisements and personal contacts or by agencies such as the **European Council of International Schools (ECIS)** and **Gabbitas, Truman & Thring.**

It is impossible to describe a typical international school. Some may have thousands of pupils, others less than a hundred. A single nationality may predominate or more than 60 different nationalities may be represented. There are schools for expatriates only, while others take in a sizeable proportion of pupils from the country in which they are located. Some are highly selective; others — particularly the American International Schools — are designed to serve children with a wide range of abilities.

Some of the main features of an international school with a high proportion of expatriate pupils are:

- **High pupil turnover.** Parents move on after finishing their contracts, and take their children with them, so there may be a lack of continuity.
- **High staff turnover.** Teachers are usually on two-year or three-year contracts. Younger ones like to move on to other countries; older ones may decide to return home before it is too late for them to resume a career there.
- **Heterogeneous clientele.** Pupils come from a variety of educational backgrounds and may return to their own educational system at a later date. The curriculum has to take into account these differing needs.
- **Varied teaching staff.** The teaching staff could well be drawn from different countries, and so misunderstandings can arise. Locally-recruited staff are often on lower salaries than staff recruited from abroad and this can give rise to tensions.

- **Disorientated pupils.** Not all children settle down easily in different schools in different environments, so teachers may need some expertise in counselling.
- **Strong parent involvement.** International schools often have strong links with the local expatriate community. Expatriate mothers with no job to occupy their attention may become very closely involved.
- **Good pupil-teacher ratios.** Compared with other schools in the country this is more than likely to be the case. It is perhaps just as well considering the heterogeneous nature of the classes.
- **Above average intelligence.** Generally speaking, people who work abroad are drawn from the higher social echelons — businessmen, diplomats, aid officials, teachers. Children often inherit their parents' traits.
- **Enhanced opportunities for education.** There are opportunities for experiencing multicultural education and for studying a new environment.

The *ECIS Directory* provides details on more than 750 primary and secondary international schools in around 140 different countries.

For international school staff there is a professional association — the **International Educator's Institute** — based in the USA. The Institute publishes a quarterly newspaper which includes vacancy listings, and offers certain perks such as insurance cover. (US address: PO Box 103, West Bridgewater, MA 02379, USA. UK office: 25 Queen Anne's Gardens, Ealing, London W5 5QD.)

The International Baccalaureate
A growing number of international schools — some 250 at present — prepare their pupils for the International Baccalaureate examination. This is a two year pre-university course designed to facilitate the mobility of students and promote international understanding. It leads to either a Diploma which is recognised by tertiary institutions in several countries, or certificates in separate subjects.

For the Diploma pupils choose one subject from each of six groups:

- Language A — usually the pupil's native tongue
- Language B — a modern foreign language or pupil's second language
- Social sciences
- Experimental sciences
- Mathematics and computing
- Art, design, music, another language, various other options.

Three of the subjects must be offered at Higher Level and three at Subsidiary Level. For example:

Higher: Mathematics, Physics, Chemistry
Subsidiary: English (A), German (B), History

Useful addresses
- The Examinations Office, International Baccalaureate, University of Bath, Claverton Down, Bath BA2 7AY (tel: 0225 62501).
- International Baccalaureate European Office, 18 Woburn Square, London WC1H 0NS (tel: 01-637 1682).

State schools

Opportunities exist for teachers in most subjects in state schools, not only in English-speaking countries but in secondary schools in countries where the second language is English.

Recruitment tends to be done by the Overseas Development Administration (ODA), the volunteer organisations, missionary societies, the British Council, and a number of private recruitment agencies. There are also teacher exchange schemes operated by the Central Bureau and the League for the Exchange of Commonwealth Teachers.

The important thing to bear in mind is that you are entering a different education system which may be founded on **different principles** from the one you have grown up with. Your duties — in the classroom and outside it — may be different. The aims of the school may be at variance with your own. Some education systems set out to teach pupils how to think and reason. Others place greater stress on learning facts. Some encourage specialisation; others go for an extremely broad curriculum. Whatever your personal views, you will need to **adapt** to the system in use.

State schools in many countries are underfunded. They have classrooms with blackboards, but there are often few, if any, facilities for practical work. This can pose problems for science and craft teachers. Even modest audio-visual aids may be hard to come by. The teacher in the state sector has to be **resourceful,** if nothing else.

Many educational systems and their protegés are obsessed by grades, not necessarily because there is a form of continuous assessment in operation. Education is seen primarily as a path to advancement where grades, certificates and diplomas are the key to future success.

The **motivation** of the pupils cannot be taken for granted. In parts of Africa where secondary education is the privilege of a few, you may well find yourself teaching bright and keen pupils. In other places there may be fewer incentives to learn.

In bilingual schools and countries where English is the second language there can be problems of **communication,** which may be puzzling to teachers who have only taught English native speakers. The onus is on the teacher to express himself more clearly and check at regular intervals that the pupils have fully understood the points made.

Another problem to contend with is **cultural differences.** In parts of Asia, for instance, it is regarded as rude to contradict the teacher, and pupils may seem irritatingly quiet and passive. Children from other cultures may expect a teacher to be authoritarian, and become disruptive if any sign of friendliness is shown. Religious custom can also affect the way pupils behave.

It is naive to envisage teaching abroad as being exactly the same as it is at home. You will have to learn a lot about the educational system you will be working in if you want your pupils to learn a lot from you!

HIGHER EDUCATION

Higher education is very much an international business, and always has been ever since the Middle Ages when the first universities came into existence. The Association of Commonwealth Universities (ACU), for instance, handles over 1,200 staff vacancies for its members each year.

Universities abroad recruit staff from Britain and elsewhere for one of two reasons:

● **By choice**
This is true, for instance, in the developed countries of the English speaking world, such as the US, Australia and New Zealand. There's no shortage of academics in these countries but universities like to have outsiders on their staff in order to stimulate an exchange of ideas and methods. They also like to recruit from a wider pool of talents than exists in their own countries. This can be achieved by the implementation of staff exchange agreements with universities in the UK and elsewhere, under which a lecturer would be seconded to a foreign institution for up to a year. More usually, though, universities actively recruit people for the long term, even to the extent of offering security of tenure.

● **Out of necessity**
Not all countries are self-sufficient in professors and lecturers, and this is particularly true of the Third World. But for many developing nations foreign expertise comes expensive — unless lecturers are employed on volunteer terms or provided free by donor governments. This means that higher education managers are keen to replace foreign staff by less expensive indigenous lecturers at the earliest possible opportunity. As a consequence, contracts tend to be fixed term only.

Demands and constraints

Any idea that service abroad is an option for lacklustre academics needs to be firmly scotched. As a result of cutbacks in higher education in the UK, **competition for posts** in universities abroad has become very keen indeed. This is particularly true in the case of tertiary institutes in the developed world which can offer ample research facilities, good salaries and often security of tenure.

Third World universities, on the other hand, operate under **financial constraints,** so that both library and research facilities may prove inadequate. However, if your area of interest is connected with the environment in which you will find yourself — tropical agriculture, the flora and fauna of the region, for example — this need not be a handicap.

Research is, of course, vital if you intend to progress in your chosen field, particularly if you are at the beginning of your career, since the profession demands that you publish on a regular basis in order to keep your name to the fore. If you are successful in doing this you should not experience difficulty in returning later to British academic life.

As for the **teaching environment,** all Commonwealth universities have grown out of the same tradition and are surprisingly homogeneous in their methods and outlook. Most new appointees are therefore able to adapt easily.

Difficulties may be experienced in other countries outside the English-speaking world, where English is used as a medium of instruction in higher education although many students lack fluency in the language. To overcome the problem lecturers may need to develop more **effective communication skills.** Foreign academics, whose native language is not English, often cope better in this area since they feel they have to try harder to overcome their linguistic handicap.

Currently there is a high demand for specialists in medicine, computer science, the natural sciences and engineering. There are very few openings for specialists in arts subjects and architecture.

3
The Job Hunt

FINDING A JOB

Once you have made the decision to work abroad, you have to start looking round for institutions that might employ you.

You could try **visiting** foreign countries on spec. Some teachers have a knack of being in the right place at the right time and manage to land first-class job offers. Or, if you have an extensive network of colleagues abroad, you could make use of the **grapevine**. Teaching contacts may be able to suggest establishments that you could apply to on a speculative basis. Names and addresses can easily be obtained from other sources as well. Alternatively, you may decide to approach **UK based agencies** which recruit for positions abroad.

The main way of learning about a teaching job abroad is through scanning the **advertisement columns** of specialist education periodicals, like the *Times Educational Supplement* and the *Times Higher Education Supplement,* certain national newspapers like the *Guardian* (Tuesday edition), or *The Times* (Monday edition). Periodicals related to your own particular discipline (such as the *Economist* or *New Scientist*) could prove a fruitful source of opportunities. Certain Church journals also carry details of vacancies abroad as do union journals, and for TEFL teachers there is the *EFL Gazette.*

VISITS ON SPEC

The advantage of actually visiting a country to find a job is that you can gain a first-hand impression of the place. You can see the educational institution and its working methods, and get an idea of the living conditions you can expect, before signing any contract.

However, while this may be a feasible option in the case of countries close to home, it can be a costly undertaking where more distant places are concerned. And there are countries that are difficult to enter unless you have specific business to undertake or are on an organised tour.

HTA—C

33

In non-EEC countries there may also be **visa difficulties.** If you enter as a tourist you may be prevented from taking up employment in the country. In order to work, you will probably need a work permit, and you can only obtain one of these if you have the appropriate visa in your passport. The process could entail leaving the country in order to obtain the required documentation for re-entry.

The **penalties** for working illegally in a country can be severe if you are caught, so it is important to check carefully first of all.

Tips

● If you are visiting a place 'on spec' remember to take evidence of your background and qualifications as well as copies of your CV.
● Before accepting a post, ask whether you are to be employed on expatriate terms or as a locally recruited staff member. Expatriate terms are usually more generous with return air fares paid to your country of origin, accommodation and other allowances.

SPECULATIVE APPLICATIONS

These may be either direct to an overseas educational institution or to a representative or agency in the UK.

Direct applications

There are a number of ways of finding the names and addresses of schools and colleges who might be interested in you.

● **Personal contacts.** Friends and colleagues overseas may be able to recommend establishments.
● **Diplomatic missions.** The Information Officer or Cultural Attaché of the appropriate High Commission, Embassy or Consulate General may be able to advise. Some missions may be able to supply you with a list of the principal educational institutions in the country concerned; others may let you consult books of reference.
● **Libraries.** Some large public reference libraries will have reference books, such as yearbooks and telephone directories from foreign countries. There are international education yearbooks such as *The World of Learning* (Europa), *The Commonwealth Universities Yearbook* (Association of Commonwealth Universities), *The ECIS Directory* (European Council of International Schools), *Learning Languages: Where and How* (Wie & Wo Verlag).
● **Education Departments** of universities, polytechnics and colleges of higher education. Many of these have links with schools and colleges in other countries and may know of vacancies. Or they

may have foreign educationists teaching or attending courses there who can advise you.

Tips

- Don't bank on getting a reply. Popular institutions are often overwhelmed by speculative applications and do not have the manpower to cope with unsolicited applications.
- You are more likely to receive a reply if you enclose an international reply coupon with your letter.

Applications to agencies and representatives

Very few agencies recruit for posts in *every* country of the world, so it makes sense to find out which country or countries they specialise in (see pages 158 and 159). Either send for details of their service or write enclosing an up-to-date CV, stating the countries and the type of work you are interested in, and asking if they know of any vacancies. They may not have vacancies then and there, but they may be willing to put your name on file, send you a vacancy list, or alert you when posts are likely to crop up.

While some agencies operate a teacher's register and welcome unsolicited letters others, such as the **Association of Commonwealth Universities (ACU),** recruit solely through advertisement, and such an approach can be counterproductive.

APPLYING FOR ADVERTISED VACANCIES

Advertisements for jobs appear all the year round, and the starting dates vary considerably, according to the academic year which differs from continent to continent, hemisphere to hemisphere. **Gabbitas, Truman & Thring,** for example, recruits between July and October for posts in the southern hemisphere, which tend to start between January and March, while their main period of recruitment for the northern hemisphere is January to May.

Don't limit yourself to newspapers and journals published in the UK. Diplomatic missions often have reading rooms where you can peruse local newspapers and so widen your choice.

AGENCIES RECRUITING TEACHERS

By far the most common method of finding a job overseas is through an agency, and you need to be aware of the various organisations working in this field, their scope, and the various schemes they operate.

Exchange schemes

The Central Bureau for Educational Visits and Exchanges and the League for the Exchange of Commonwealth Teachers should be mentioned in the context of opportunities to work abroad, although they are not in the business of *recruiting* teachers for long-term engagements. Teachers undertake **exchanges** for reasons of professional development and return to teaching within the UK at the end of their term.

The **Central Bureau** offers educational exchanges of up to a year to Europe and the USA for experienced and qualified teachers. In addition, it administers a large foreign assistantship exchange scheme for modern languages undergraduates and recent graduates. There are opportunities not only in Europe, but in French-speaking Canada, Latin America, and a few countries in Africa.

The **League** sends about 250 teachers overseas each year, mostly to Australia, Canada and New Zealand. The preferred age range is 25-45.

The **Japan Exchange and Teaching Programme** more or less fits into this category though there is no reciprocal exchange. Administered by Gabbitas, Truman & Thring and the Japanese Embassy it sends around 150 would-be TEFL teachers a year to work in Japanese schools and with local educational authorities.

Public agencies

The British Council operates cultural centres in many countries throughout the world, and recruits up to 500 people per year for contract posts mainly in TEFL. The main types of posts are

- ODA-sponsored posts, formerly known as Key English Language Teaching (KELT) posts. These are senior posts, often in universities, teacher training institutes and ministries of education.
- Posts in the Council's own language schools (DTEOs) — over 50 in number operating in some 45 countries.
- Posts in Communist bloc countries. The British Council is often the only organsiation recruiting for such countries. The positions are usually at the tertiary level, and may well be subsidised.
- Posts for which the Council operates solely as a recruitment agency. In recent years the organisation has recruited for schools in Hong Kong, Botswana and Latin America, and on behalf of other organisations round the world.

The Overseas Development Administration (ODA) recruits for countries in the Middle East, Arica, Latin America, the Far East and Pacific. Teaching appointments come under the Overseas Service Aid Scheme (OSAS) or the British Expatriates' Supplementation Scheme whereby the British Government tops up the local salary and offers other inducements. Technical co-operation appointments are funded completely by ODA.

The ODA also recruits on behalf of international agencies, such as the World Bank, UNIDO, OECD and the European Community, through its International Recruitment Unit.

Interview Fund. Teachers serving abroad recruited by either the British Council or ODA may be eligible for a reimbursement of part of their travel costs if they need to return to the UK in connection with an interview for an appointment towards the end of their service overseas.

The Service Children's Education Authority (SCEA) recruits for service schools all over the world and operates in the same way as a local education authority in the UK, except that positions are offered on a contract basis.

Volunteer agencies

The largest of these agencies is **Voluntary Service Overseas** which operates in more than 40 Third World countries and recruits more than 250 teachers annually. The average age of a volunteer is 30 and some are in their sixties. There are posts in most subjects in all educational sectors, including special education.

Accommodation and payment based on local rates are provided by the community, organisation or government requesting volunteers. VSO for its part provides training and pays for air fares, national insurance, medical insurance and equipment grants. 'Every volunteer . . . often leaves secure employment in the UK with little anticipation of any real material reward for the two years' tough and unpredictable experience ahead', says a VSO brochure. The organisation recruits for posts in Africa, the Caribbean, China, SE Asia and the Pacific.

VSO recruits on behalf of **United Nations Volunteers.** The other agencies are **International Voluntary Service** (IVS) which works mainly in Botswana, Lesotho, Mozambique and Swaziland — and the **Catholic Institute for International Relations** (CIIR). The **United Nations Association** also has a volunteer programme (UNAIS) and runs an unofficial volunteer co-ordinating committee to which all volunteer recruitment agencies belong.

Private sector agencies

Perhaps the oldest established agency of its kind is **Gabbitas, Truman**

& Thring which recruits mainly primary and secondary school teachers for private English-medium schools in most parts of the world.

The Centre for British Teachers (CBT) on the other hand, recruits teachers for its own projects and employs them directly. Most of the posts on offer are in state secondary schools in Germany, Brunei, Malaysia and Oman. In most cases a few years' experience is required.

Other agencies are listed in **Useful Addresses, p.160.**

Language school recruitment agencies

There are a number of these. Some actually own the schools for which they recruit, while others are just acting as recruitment agencies, so when approaching such an agency find out what the precise relationship is. The following are two typical examples.

International House recruits world-wide for 70 independent language schools and teacher training institutes affiliated to the International House Trust, especially in Spain, Portugal and Italy. Teaching posts within the organisation are suitable for single people and married couples with no dependants. The minimum qualification is the RSA Preparatory Certificate with a Pass A or Pass B (which can be studied at IH's Teacher Training Institute), though preference is always given to people with teaching experience as well. There are also opportunities at a more senior level for suitably experienced and qualified people.

Inlingua is a Swiss owned organisation of independent private language schools, most of which operate in Germany, Italy and Spain. Graduates in all specialisms are considered, and those without TEFL qualifications will be expected to enrol on a short training course in the Inlingua method.

Church and missionary agencies

Christians Abroad is an organisation funded largely by aid agencies and mission agencies to provide information, counselling and general support for people seeking work abroad. It also recruits teachers in its own right — not necessarily to mission establishments — and publishes on a regular basis an extensive bulletin of vacancies abroad for which its member agencies (all 37 of them) are recruiting.

In general, missionary societies are not looking for teachers but lay missionaries with teaching qualifications. Their main purpose is to proclaim the gospel, and most are not really into an extensive teacher recruitment programme.

Some of the older established agencies operate through a system of recommendation, and the first point of contact for a lay missionary is likely to be a parish priest or chaplain.

However, some, like the **Volunteer Missionary Movement,** do advertise their vacancies in journals from time to time, and many use the vacancies bulletin put out by Christians Abroad.

Other agencies

The Association of Commonwealth Universities

The Association (which does not deal with unsolicited applications) advertises posts on behalf of its 312 member universities in the press and specialist journals, and also circulates vacancies to university registrars and careers advisory services. The largest number of vacancies are for institutions in Australia, Botswana, Brunei, Hong Kong, Lesotho, New Zealand, Papua New Guinea, Fiji, Swaziland, West Indies, Zimbabwe and Malaysia. The ACU interviews candidates on behalf of its member institutions if asked to do so, and sends off individual reports which are designed to help the institution in question come to an informed decision. The Association has no hand in either the shortlisting or the final outcome, and does not act as a mediator between its members and their appointees. The ACU publishes a useful source of reference, *The Commonwealth Universities Handbook*.

The European Council of International Schools

The ECIS operates a teachers' register and charges a small membership fee. It recruits for primary and secondary schools throughout the world which, generally speaking, offer a British style or American style curriculum. The number of teaching opportunities outside Europe is currently on the increase. One feature of the ECIS programme is a two-day recruitment fair held in London every February which brings together around 300 candidates and representatives of over 70 schools throughout the world, but recruitment continues throughout the year, the busy period being from February to May.

Embassies

Teacher recruitment is also conducted by embassies, high commissions and other diplomatic missions based in London, usually for posts in the state secondary and tertiary sector. Among the countries which have used this method of recruitment in recent years are Ghana, Nigeria, Singapore and Sudan.

Companies operating overseas

British Aerospace is one of a number of companies which has a contract to supply both hardware and a training package. In Saudi Arabia, for example, the company employs personnel to train pilots and ground-staff, and this includes English language tuition. A number of other companies, in the oil and hospital sectors particularly, are also heavily involved in training. In some cases the company does its own recruitment, but more often than not a recruitment agency is asked to do the work.

This is a brief survey of the types of agencies involved in teacher recruitment and not a definitive list. There are many other organisations of considerable repute — especially in the TEFL field. All of them fall into one of the various categories listed above and most are listed in the appendix.

THE APPLICATION PROCEDURE

The fact that you have discovered a job vacancy does not mean that it is automatically yours. Competition can be very keen for some of the more attractive posts, and the successful candidate is the one who can give a good account of himself (or herself).

Remember that the application process itself is time-consuming. True, there are cases where a person finds himself jetting towards his destination within days of the interview, but they are very much the exception.

HOW THE OVERSEAS RECRUITMENT PROCESS WORKS

This is a typical example of recruitment procedures when a third party (ie a recruitment agency) is involved. When you are dealing direct with prospective employers some of the stages do not apply.

1. Agency receives request to fill a vacancy from institution abroad.
2. Agency advertises the position or circulates information about it.
3. Candidate sees advertisement and sends off for details.
4. Agency sends the candidate a job description and an application form.
5. Candidate sends in application.
6. Agency selects suitable candidates for interview.
7. Agency contacts referees. (This may occur either before or after the interview.)
8. Candidate receives invitation to an interview.
9. Candidate confirms that he can attend for interview.
10. Agency interviews candidate (in some cases there may be two interviews: a preliminary interview followed by an in-depth one, perhaps with the prospective employer, at a later date).
11. Candidate receives letter from agency to say whether he has been successful. If so, his name will be passed on to the institution for approval.
12. Candidate confirms that he is still interested in the post.
13. Agency sends off candidate's details for approval by the institution.

14. Institution considers candidate's details. (In some cases the institution has to submit the candidate's particulars for government approval, otherwise it may be difficult to get an entry visa or work permit.)
15. Agency receives go-ahead from institution to appoint the candidate.
16. Agency contacts candidate to confirm appointment.
17. Candidate visits agency for briefing and to sign contract.

As you will see, this is quite an involved procedure, and hiccups can occur anywhere along the line. If the advertisement fails to attract a reasonable number of candidates, the post may well be re-advertised (stage 2). Interviews may have to be delayed for the sake of candidates from overseas (stage 10). There may be delay in getting official approval (stage 14). Even if things go smoothly, the whole process could take two to three months, and even at the end of it all, you may not be appointed.

YOUR APPLICATION

The letter of application
This is your first point of contact with the agency or employer and since first impressions count, you have got to impress. In these competitive times it has to amount to more than just a covering letter. You need to convey:

● I'm interested . . . in the post.
● I can do the job . . . I have the right qualifications and just the experience you are looking for.
● I'm available . . . to attend for interview/to start . . .

The letter has to be

● **Neat** — on A4 paper, preferably typed, unless your handwriting is impeccable.
● **Concise** — don't write more than five crisp paragraphs.
● **Relevant** — mention aspects of your experience which make you well-suited to the post in question.
● **Enthusiastic** — show that you really want the job.

Think of those wonderful blurbs that you see on the jackets of books. Your letter in its modest way serves the same purpose. It has got to make you wanted (see p.42). A speculative letter of application needs to be in a similar vein, but instead of targeting on a particular job you will need to mention a broader range of experience (see p.43).

Tel ....   82 Cawdor Place
                                                  Dundee
                                                  Scotland

                                                  30 May 1989

Director of Recruitment
Macduff International
12 Duncan Road
Dunsinane
DU5 9ZQ

Dear Sir

I wish to apply for the post of Teacher of Science at St Andrew's
International School in Bulawayo, as advertised in this week's
Scottish Educational Review.

I am most interested in this post, firstly — because it sounds
varied and challenging, secondly — because I wish to extend my
experience, and thirdly — because I am a fervent believer in the
idea of international education.

Since graduation I have worked in the state sector of education,
teaching physics and chemistry up to 'A' level standard. I am
happy to say that during this period we achieved a 90% pass rate
in all subjects.

Last year I started a pilot scheme designed to establish closer links
between my school and local industry by means of factory visits.
The project has been so successful that sixth formers will have a
chance to gain practical experience in company laboratories during
the next 12 months.

I am Secretary of the regional branch of the Association of
Science Teachers, and am currently working on an elementary
science workbook for Africa.

I would welcome a chance to meet you to discuss the post in
depth.

Yours faithfully

Banquo MacBeth

Model Letter of Application

Tel ....   P.O. Box 100
                                                           Mandalay
                                                           Burma

                                                           24 September 1988

Principal
Atlantic University
Funchal
Madeira

Dear Sir

I am writing to enquire whether you have any vacancies in your
English Department, preferably with effect from the beginning of
next year when my contract at the Kipling Teacher Training
Institute comes to an end.

I have an MA in English and Linguistics from Tara University in
the USA, and have spent some 15 years overseas in the field of
English language teaching, and teacher training. During that time I
have written a number of learned papers as well as a textbook,
Speak English like a Native, which has been approved for use in
schools by the Ministry of Education of Vanuatu.

Having worked in Brazil over a number of years I am familiar
with the language learning problems of Portuguese speakers. I am
also a fluent Portuguese speaker myself, and have visited Lisbon
on two occasions to address teacher training conferences. I have
also taught in Mauritania, Liechtenstein and Ecuador.

I do so hope that you will be able to give me a positive reply. I
enclose an international reply coupon.

Yours sincerely

Sean O'Hara

Model Speculative Letter

Curriculum Vitae

A good CV takes time to prepare whether you are at the beginning of your teaching career or have many years' experience behind you. Take time over it. Make copious notes of your achievements and then start to whittle them down so that you can accommodate everything on a sheet of A4. Pages 45 and 46 show examples of typical CVs.

A CV needs to be typed and to look good. If you can't type yourself, ask a professional to do the job for you, preferably on a word-processor so that it can be edited.

Although it is a factual document, it offers you a chance to blow your own trumpet. Draw attention to your successes, but not your failures.

- **Personal details.** Name, address, telephone number, age, nationality. You don't necessarily have to put in items like marital status, dependants or religion.

- **Education.** Educational institutions, dates attended, examinations passed. You don't need to go into detail about your O Level results if you left school decades ago.

- **Summary of work experience.** This is optional, but it gives you an opportunity to list your strengths and accomplishments.

- **Employment record (or career).** List posts held and organisations worked for with approximate dates. There is no need to disclose reasons for leaving or the salary you earned. Give a concise description of your responsibilities for each post. Go into more detail if you have opted to leave out the summary of work experience. Use words which are likely to impress like 'initiate', 'expand', 'introduce', 'achieve', 'exceed'. Every selector appreciates dynamism. If you have recently graduated, remember to include vacation employment.

- **Interests and activities.** List memberships of clubs, societies, professional bodies, including any posts of responsibility you hold or have held in them. Don't list too many, otherwise you may give the impression that you won't have enough time to cope with a job!

- **Other information.** This is where you include other skills not yet mentioned such as language ability, possession of a driving licence, or other information, such as your DES number (if you have one).

Application form

'Is the application form really necessary?' is a question that passes through the minds of many candidates. If you have sent in a comprehen-

Curriculum Vitae
HELEN TROY

Address: 2 Paris Close, Priamsville, Hectorshire HS12 3ZY
Telephone: 10 234 5678 (daytime); 9087 654321 (evenings and weekends)
Date of Birth: 1st January 1966
Nationality: British   *Marital Status:* Single

EDUCATION AND QUALIFICATIONS
1977-1984   Dido Park Comprehensive, Minervathorpe, London W29 9XV
            GCE 'O' Level 1982:
            English Language (A); Latin (A); History (B); Mathematics (B);
            Sociology (B); Greek (C); Biology (C)
            GCE 'A' Level 1984:
            Latin (A); Russian (A); Sociology (C)

1984-1987   University of Carthage
            BA Hons in Linguistics and Philosophy (Lower Second) 1987

1987-1988   Hades Polytechnic
            Postgraduate Certificate of Education (Latin and TEFL)

WORK EXPERIENCE
Summer 1985   Organiser, YMCA Holiday Camp for the Disabled, Lake
              Tarquin
Summer 1986   Relief Manageress, Juno Ladies' Wear, Spartaham
Summer 1987   Social organiser, Lethe Summer School for Foreign
              Students, Styx
August 1988   Supply Teacher with Cassandrashire Education Authority
onwards   I have undertaken a number of assignments with the
              authority notably teaching remedial English to
              immigrants, French to 'O' Level standard, and General
              Studies

INTERESTS AND ACTIVITIES
Hang Gliding: I was Treasurer of the Hades Poly Hang Gliding Club
Amateur Dramatics: While at university I acted in several productions,
                   including 'Charley's Aunt' and 'Cat on a Hot Tin
                   Roof', and directed 'Oedipus Rex'
Mountaineering
Music: I play the French Horn

OTHER INFORMATION
I have a clean driving licence.
I am currently attending evening classes in Italian and hope to take
   'O' Level this coming summer.
In addition to speaking Russian, I know some Spanish and Bulgarian.

John C. Falstaff — Career History

Home Address: 16 Bardolph Court, Windsor, Berks
Address for correspondence: P.O. Box 2, Ulan Bator, Outer Mongolia
Date of Birth: 31st December 1938
Nationality: Australian   *Family Status:* Married with 6 children

Educational Record
1949-1957   Arden Forest Grammar School
              5 'O' Levels; 'A' Level in Biology, Physics and Anatomy
1960-1964   Warwick University, NSW, Australia
              BSc Hons in Comparative Botany (First Class)
1964-1969   Agincourt University, Hotspur, USA
              PhD in Botanical Studies

Professional Experience
TEACHING AND LECTURING
    I have taught Botany and Applied Biology to Master's Degree level and supervised research graduates in these fields.

RESEARCH
    I have conducted research studies on three continents, and have been published in numerous journals over the years. My 800 page study on the Tanzanian lesser spotted orchid is regarded as a milestone in botanical research. (A list of my publications is appended to this document.)

ADMINISTRATION
    As a former assistant head of a botanical research establishment I have plenty of experience of managing people and coping with red tape.

Career Details
1957-1958   Management Trainee, Boar's Head Hotels, Sydney
1958-1960   Quality Control Manager, Boar's Head Hotels
1969-1975   Lecturer in Botany, Eastcheap Polytechnic
1975-1976   Adviser to the Ministry of Agriculture, Republic of Ruritania
1976-1979   Senior Lecturer in Biology, Eastcheap Polytechnic
1983-1985   Deputy Director, Botanical Research Establishment, Alice Springs
1985-1988   Acting Head of Botany Department, Eastcheap Polytechnic
1988-   Currently doing research into the flora of Outer Mongolia on
              a fellowship awarded by the Mongolian Institute of Sciences

Interests and Hobbies
Croquet, Billiards, Sailing and Jazz

Additional Information
During recent years I have also held a number of part-time and honorary
    positions:
Member of the Crumhorn Commission on the Countryside (UK)
Consultant to the Irish Universities Board
Chairman of the Orchid Development Board of Australia

sive CV, filling in another form seems a waste of time. Besides, it may be difficult to accommodate your details on it.

If the agency/employer considers it necessary, then you have no option but to fill it in. If the vacancy attracts a large number of candidates it is much easier for the selectors to compare them if their details are in a standardised format. To complete only half the form may suggest that you are half-hearted about the post.

An application form needs to be approached with respect, otherwise the completed article may turn out to be a mess. So:

- **Read it through** to find out what information is wanted.
- **Make notes** on how you will fill in each section.
- **Fill it in** slowly and clearly following the instructions carefully.

The **personal details** section is fairly straightforward. Don't forget to include a telephone number (that of a neighbour, friend or relative will do if you don't have one of your own), the selectors may need to contact you urgently during office hours.

When filling in your **educational details** don't put in bogus information — it may be checked. Include details of any short courses you may have done recently to show that you like to keep on top of your subject.

Your record of **work experience** should include all jobs even if they have nothing to do with teaching. This applies particularly if you are near the beginning of your career.

If your work experience is extensive devote more space to jobs you have held in recent years. If you are required to mention your reasons for leaving a job, and you are uneasy about disclosing information, write 'To be discussed at interview'. Don't do this too often, though — the selectors might become suspicious.

Ideally your **referees** should be based in the British Isles, or at least one of them should be. Make sure you choose people who know you well and can give a good account of you and keep them informed of your career developments. Check that they are willing to do the chore. There are three types of referee which could be required:

- **Academic:** If you have completed a course within the last five years or so this will be your tutor or Head of Department. If you haven't, ignore this requirement, unless you happen to have kept in very close touch with your *alma mater*.

- **Personal:** This is someone who has known you for several years, and who can vouch for your honesty and integrity. A friend, but not a relative, is quite acceptable. Don't go in for an eminent person for the sake of effect, unless he or she knows you well enough to give a convincing reference.

● **Professional:** This will normally be your present employer or head of department. If you don't want them to be contacted, choose someone you have worked for or under in the past. If you have worked abroad in a goverment subsidised post, someone in the British Council or Embassy who knows your work may be an acceptable substitute.

Good general advice would be: Try to answer every question honestly. If it doesn't apply to you write N/A (not applicable) in the space. Do follow instructions to the letter. IF BLOCK LETTERS are specified, write in block letters. Some forms specify black ink or typescript, for example, to facilitate photocopying.

THE INTERVIEW

Your endeavours so far have been pitched at securing an interview. The purpose of the interview is to secure the job, and having reached this stage you are in with a chance. However, many people regard the interview as a nerve-racking affair, where their fate hangs in the balance.

Remember, you are going to be in the spotlight, and so, like any performer, you need to prepare yourself for the ordeal:

● read up about the job, country and organisation you will be working for
● list the qualities and experience you could bring to the job
● try to envisage what kind of person the organisation wants
● note down the type of questions you expect the selectors to ask
● decide how you might answer the questions, particularly the tricky ones
● think up some questions that you would like to ask about the job
● get in some interview practice.

In a word you have to **sell yourself.** This means being knowledgeable about the product (yourself), your client and his needs, and being able to handle the interview effectively, always drawing attention to your eminent suitability for the post. This is a tall order. Don't worry though. No interviewee is perfect.

Dos and don'ts at the interview

● arrive in good time
● endeavour to create a favourable impression right from the start
● try to establish some rapport with the interviewer

- be positive about your achievements
- display enthusiasm
- keep calm
- ask the interviewer to repeat a question if you haven't understood it
- be as natural as you can in the circumstances.

On the other hand:

- don't sit down until invited to
- don't make exaggerated claims
- don't argue with the interviewer or interrupt him
- don't draw attention to your weaknesses by trying to justify yourself
- don't make jokes
- don't run down your present or past employers
- don't ramble on.

After some time you may be invited to ask some questions. Don't assume that the interview is over at that moment. You are still in the business of making an impact, so don't spoil your chances by mounting a detailed investigation into salary and conditions unless this crops up during the course of the interview.

Suggested questions

When do you hope to make an appointment?
To whom will I be responsible?
When will I be expected to start?
What sort of textbooks does the institution use?
What educational aids will be available at post?
Who actually issues the contract and can I see a copy?
What facilities do you offer in the way of briefing?

Don't expect to get precise answers, particularly if the organisation is acting merely as an agent.

A final word — don't forget that you are likely to be competing with a goodly number of well qualified and keen candidates. And don't make the mistake of underestimating the standard of application which the better candidates will undoubtedly be making.

4
The Decision to Go

MAKING UP YOUR MIND

When you receive a firm offer of a job overseas, you need to make up your mind fairly quickly. However, a number of teachers come to grief every year because they make up their minds *too* quickly. Going to work abroad is a much bigger step than going to work in an adjacent county, and you must take nothing for granted. Working conditions and living conditions aren't going to be precisely as they are back home. Even if you only venture as far as Calais, you will find yourself in a different environment, and this can bother some people if they come unprepared.

The onus is on you — and you alone — to find out in advance what you are letting yourself in for *before* you sign your contract. There is little point in taking up a post unless it satisfies at least some of your aspirations — in areas such as remuneration, experience, job satisfaction, status, for instance.

SOURCES OF INFORMATION AND ADVICE

The employer or recruitment agency
When you apply for a position, many organisations will provide you with a detailed job description and notes on living conditions in the country. The interview is another opportunity to learn about what is on offer so make a list of relevant questions in advance. The final opportunity to gather information will be when you are actually offered the job, when you may have cause to query certain aspects of your contract — and perhaps negotiate changes.

Libraries
The reference sections of most larger public libraries will have handbooks on different countries or regions of the world, ranging from guidebooks to briefings for businessmen. An encyclopedia might be a good starting point.

Lending libraries will usually have a number of books dealing with specific countries but for information on education in different countries it might be better to consult a specialist educational library belonging to a university or institute of higher education, such as the London University Institute of Education's Library at 11-13 Ridgmount Street, London WC1 (tel: 01-637 0846).

Foreign embassies, high commissions and consulates

A number of embassies, high commissions and consulates (particularly those of western countries) have information packs on living conditions. If not, there may be an information officer who is willing to answer your questions or supply you with some information on the country. Many will be able to supply you with tourist brochures, usually issued free, or even perhaps maps. Bear in mind, though, that these are designed to show the country in the best possible light rather than to provide a down-to-earth assessment of the living conditions you will experience. If the diplomatic mission does not have any literature of this nature, there may well be a national tourist office or national airline office in London (or in other cities) that does.

The British Council and other public bodies

The British Council has an English Teaching Information Centre (ETIC) at its headquarters at 10 Spring Gardens, London SW1A 2BN (tel: 01-930 8466 ext. 2783 and 2350). The Centre is not open to the casual visitor. The staff can answer telephone and written enquiries, but if you wish to browse through the bookshelves, make an appointment first. The Centre also publishes English teaching profiles of many countries.

The Foreign and Commonwealth Office and Overseas Development Administration may also be able to provide information.

Specialist organisations

- The Centre for International Briefing, Farnham Castle, Surrey GU9 0AG (tel: 0252 721194) organises a regular programme of briefings on different parts of the world for people due to take up postings abroad. The courses are residential and usually of four days' duration. Some employers (notably ODA) offer their recruits an option to attend such a course, but the majority do not. The Centre has an extensive library of books, videos, cassettes, reports and other material on virtually every country in the world, including many personal accounts. Non-course members may use it on a fee-paying basis. There is also a well stocked bookshop in the building which offers a mail order service for customers who cannot make a personal visit.

- Expatriate Briefings, Rectory Road, Great Waldingfield, Sudbury, Suffolk CO10 0TL (tel: 0787 78607) produces notes on individual countries with advice on health, education, finance, etc.
- Country reports are also provided by *Inside Tracks,* a monthly publication from Christopher Woodley, 10 Hartswood Road, London W12 2GQ, and Employment Conditions Abroad, see p.163.
- Expats International, 62 Tritton Road, London SE21 8DE (tel: 01-670 8304) is an independent organisation established in 1979 which provides assistance, information and support to working expatriates, and has a membership of over 8,000.
- The Women's Corona Society, Minster House, 274 Vauxhall Bridge Road, London SW1V 1BB (tel: 01-828 1652) provides one day briefings and publishes *Notes for Newcomers* on various countries.
- Agency for Personal Service Overseas, 29 Fitzwilliam Square, Dublin 2.
- Christians Abroad, 11 Carteret Street, London SW1H 9DL (tel: 01-222 2165).

Useful information will also be obtainable from your union or the Overseas Contract Teachers and Advisers Branch of the IPCS — the Institution of Professional Civil Servants. OCTAB's membership currently consists largely of teachers recruited by the British Council, but also has a small number of staff working for ODA and private teaching organisations. The Branch has negotiating rights only with the Council and indirectly with the ODA but can provide advice on a number of matters as well as a wide range of personal benefits and services. (Address: IPCS, 75-79 York Road, London SE1 7AQ.)

A personal inspection

The best way to find out about the position is to have a look at the establishment and the country first of all. Very few organisations will actually be prepared to fund a personal reconaissance, but if it is not too far away, it could be worth making a brief trip. By talking to people on the spot you will be in a much better position to assess the situation than if you rely on second-hand or third-hand reports.

MATTERS FOR CONSIDERATION

Accommodation

Teaching abroad is not without its frustrations, and sometimes at the end of the day you will need a shell in which to curl up and recuperate. Adequate accommodation should therefore rank high on your list of priorities. And it is important to be clear what provision is to be made before you sign the contract. Generally speaking the higher the salary, the better the standard of accommodation — and *vice versa*. But this does not always follow.

Accommodation provided can vary enormously. You could find yourself housed in a modern villa with a communal swimming pool, or in spartan quarters consisting of only one room. If you are teaching at a boarding establishment, you may find that you also have supervisory responsibilities.

You will need to ask:

- What standard of accommodation can I expect?
- Do I have any choice in the matter?
- Is it furnished, and if not, do I get a furniture allowance?
- Are any deductions made from my salary as a contribution to the cost?
- What services do I have to pay for? (electricity, concierge, etc)
- How adequately furnished will the accommodation be?
- Will I move in immediately on arrival?

Rent allowance is good from one point of view in that you have some choice in the matter of accommodation, but you need to ensure that it will be adequate. And remember you are talking about rented **furnished** accommodation. Unfurnished accommodation is out of the question unless you are also receiving a furniture allowance. There is no point in taking your Chesterfield sofa to the other side of the world. The important questions in this case will be:

- What type of accommodation will the allowance provide?
- How easy is it to find?
- Will the rent allowance cover any premium/deposit I may have to pay?
- Will I receive any assistance in finding accommodation?
- Will the contract be signed with me or my employer? (the latter is preferable)
- What accommodation provision is there for me on arrival?

There may be **no accommodation provision** or allowance. This is particularly likely in Europe. You will need to make sure that your salary will be adequate to pay for reasonable accommodation. Bear in mind that it could be expensive and scarce in capital cities and university towns. Try to find out the likely cost of accommodation, whether you can get help in finding it and whether a salary advance might be made to cover any deposit.

Financial and contractual matters

Your contract should set out details of your remuneration, but the implications should be checked carefully. A fairly modest salary can look much more attractive if it is free of tax and is likely to be supplemented by bonuses and payments made for extra duties. On the other hand, what looks like a first-class salary may work out less attractive where you have to pay for your own accommodation and the cost of living is astronomical. Have the following questions in mind when considering financial and contractual matters:

- How does the salary compare with that of local teachers and other expatriates?
- Is the salary taxable? If so, how much tax must I pay?
- Are there any allowances payable? (eg for dependants)
- Is any provision made for contributions to pension funds or national insurance contributions?
- Is my salary paid in local currency and, if so, is it transferable into other currencies?
- What deductions are made, and can they be reclaimed?
- What penalties are there for premature termination of contract?
- Is there a terminal gratuity or any other form of bonus?
- What provision is made for health care and sick pay?
- What are the travel arrangements to the post? Do I have any choice in the matter?

Some contracts tend to be vague and brief, and can lead to misunderstandings, particularly if verbal promises are made which are not incorporated into the text. A detailed contract which lays down the obligations of both employee and employer is therefore preferable, unless you have a longstanding relationship with a particular organisation and know it to be trustworthy.

Teachers sometimes find that they are expected to sign one contract with the recruitment agency and a second contract on arrival at post which may contain different conditions. This is not necessarily due to malevolence on the employer's part, but could be merely to satisfy local employment laws. You should, however, ask for clarification on this matter and an outline of the terms of the local contract.

If you have any reservations as to what you are signing, consult a solicitor, your union or the Overseas Contract Teachers' Association (see p.52).

Living conditions

Apart from financial and professional considerations you need to investigate whether life is going to be worth living. If you place great value on your lifestyle or have dependants who will accompany you, amenities are going to be important.

Not only do you want an idea as to what is available, you also need to know whether you can afford it. If you are a keen golfer, for example, you will not be able to play golf in Japan on a teacher's salary. Use the following list of questions as a guide to the sort of things you need to find out about your future lifestyle:

- How does the cost of living compare with that of the UK?
- What is the inflation rate?
- What are the shopping facilities like?
- What items, if any, are in short supply?
- Are imports freely available?
- Do I have any duty free import privileges?
- What recreational facilities are there?
- What is service like?
- Is domestic help readily available?
- What is public transport like?
- How vital is it to have your own car?
- How many expatriates live in the area?
- What kind of a social life do people have?
- What cultural amenities (libraries, cinemas, theatre) are there?

Social and political climate

All other countries are foreign but some are more foreign than others. People can feel uneasy in their new environment, and the unease may increase with the passing of time. You may find the regime autocratic and oppressive, or be alarmed at the gross disparity between rich and poor. You may find that religious taboos are restricting your social life.

The proportion of genuine democracies in the world is relatively small and, much as you may wish to increase that number, as a foreigner you shouldn't attempt to influence political events within your host country. You'll need to turn a blind eye to certain matters and exercise discretion in your pronouncements.

Teachers generally have much more contact with local people than other expatriates, diplomats, for example, and are less insulated from the world outside. Some have difficulty in coming to terms with their new environment, while others are born survivors who never make a false step.

You may find in time that — as at home — some people are sensitive to criticism, unwilling to mix with foreigners, just plain dishonest, or whatever. While I have found most foreign nationals both considerate and accommodating to foreigners, it is as well to note these possibilities in advance.

In seeking to understand the culture, bear in mind, too, that the status of women will vary from country to country. Try to ascertain from the start what subjects are taboo and how cautious you need to be in expressing opinions.

You will also, of course, want to find out what the government of the country is like and what effect the political situation has on people's lives.

Working conditions

It is just as well to know exactly what will be expected of you. Don't assume that the same conditions apply in education throughout the world. In some cases you just need to turn up for your lessons or lectures. In other establishments you are expected to be in position from before the beginning of the school day till after the end of it. You may find that you are expected to be involved in out of school activities, like parents' meetings or students' clubs.

Be clear in your mind as to your obligations to your employer and his obligations to you. This will avoid disappointment and potential disputes when you arrive.

Many detailed questions will need to be answered, including the following:

- How many class contact hours will I have per week?
- Will I receive payment for extra hours worked?
- Will I have other responsibilities, for instance, for administration, testing or counselling?
- What are the dates of the academic year?
- During which hours and days will I be expected to be on site?
- What is my leave entitlement and will holiday pay be due in advance or in arrears?
- Are there any restrictions on outside activities, such as private teaching or consultancy?
- Are there any published guidelines for teachers?

Family considerations

Even if you are quite happy to go off to some distant clime, if you have dependants then family considerations will loom large. You have three options:

- Take them with you.
- Take your spouse with you and leave the children at home either in the care of a relative or friend, or in a boarding school.
- Leave the whole family at home and strike out on your own.

Option 1

There is a lot to be said for having your family about you. They will offer you moral support and comfort and help overcome any sense of strangeness that you feel. If your children are young, there is usually no problem with their education but once they reach secondary level there may be no suitable school for them in your overseas location. The *ECIS Directory* can provide information as to whether there is.

Option 2

This is a solution followed by a number of families, particularly diplomats. Your children will be able to join you on holiday, or you can arrange for your home leave to coincide with theirs. Which of the two options you choose will depend on your children. If they have reached a critical point in their school career, it might be unwise to move them, and you will want to look into ways of keeping them at home, perhaps with a relation or close family friend who will keep an eye on their progress. A boarding school education may be a very good solution for the right kind of child but, unless you are offered an allowance towards the cost of their education, the cost could prove prohibitive.

Option 3

In some cases this is the only option. Bachelor status posts are quite normal in the Middle East, and separation is often compensated for by generous leave entitlements and high tax-free salaries. However, if you are a closely knit family lengthy absences can cause problems at home, and you will naturally discuss the implications with your family before signing the contract.

It has to be admitted that overseas postings, whether accompanied or unaccompanied, can put considerable strain on marriages. In a foreign location your partner could be bored to death with having nothing to do, or fail to adapt readily to the new surroundings. Partners who are used to pursuing an active career may become frustrated if they are prevented from taking up employment by local labour laws.

According to Expats International (see p.52) prolonged separation is a frequent cause of marital break up. Posts offering bachelor-status terms are therefore more appropriate for single people and divorcees than for married people, unless the marital relationship happens to be exceptionally resilient.

Wives Abroad, written and published by Cecilia Leong Salobir (Mayenfischstrasse 19, D7750 Konstanz, W. Germany) and available from the Castle Bookshop, Farnham Castle, is essential reading for women who will be accompanying their husbands to Third World countries.

One final matter is what to do with family pets? In some cases you may be able to take them with you, but on return to this country they will need to go into quarantine. In any case, pets tend to be reluctant expatriates. The RSPCA or a similar animal welfare society should be able to advise.

CHECKLIST

This is a summary of the main points you need to be clear about when you sign your contract.

- [ ] What is the name and address of the employer?
- [ ] Where exactly will I be employed?
- [ ] What is my job title?
- [ ] What exactly does the job involve?
- [ ] What is the normal period of notice if either side wishes to terminate the contract?
- [ ] Is the contract renewable?
- [ ] Is there a probationary period, and if so, for how long?
- [ ] What will my net earnings be and what is my tax liability at post?
- [ ] What are the arrangements for absence due to sickness?
- [ ] If I have to leave before completion of contract will the return fare be paid?
- [ ] Are my qualifications acceptable in the country where I shall be working?
- [ ] What is the procedure for acquiring a visa or work permit?
- [ ] What help can I count on in the event of a contractual disagreement?
- [ ] What perks are there? (eg free transport, pension fund, commissary privileges, duty free privileges)

PREPARING TO GO

Happy the man or woman who can traverse the world living out of a suitcase! If you are someone with few possessions, no ties and no responsibilities, moving to a distant clime can be a very simple matter. If you have a house, a family and a few trappings of wealth, a move can prove much more traumatic.

Banking

You will probably want to visit your bank before you leave to:

- inform them of your move and leave a contact address.
- obtain foreign exchange, etc, for your journey and to tide you over the initial stages of your stay abroad.
- arrange for a transfer of money to a bank abroad. (This may not be necessary if you are assured of an advance of salary on arrival.)
- obtain a letter of introduction to a bank in the town where you will be working. (This is not always vital, as your employer may be able to do this for you. In any case, you may have no need to, or may not wish to, use a bank abroad.)
- arrange to have your various financial commitments (rates, mortgage etc) paid by standing order to reduce paperwork. (If you do not plan to remit your salary to the account, you need to arrange for the account to be topped up. Bear in mind that international bank transfers are not always speedy.)
- avail yourself of your bank's advisory services (see p.65).

Car

Some employers will assist teachers in the purchase and shipping of a car, and this is a perk that you should take advantage of, since you can order a duty free car in British at a considerable saving on the normal showroom price. Do check, however, that it will not be subject to a heavy duty at the other end. It is best to go for a model which is fairly common in the country where you will be working and for which there is a local agent, otherwise you may have problems with spares and servicing.

Heavy duty suspension and perhaps a low compression engine are advisable for many Third World countries. Remember, too, that countries expect cars to comply with certain national standards, for example on exhaust emissions. Car distributors that specialise in export sales should be able to advise you on this score.

If you don't want to splash out too much, you could rely on your own car, but subject it to a thorough overhaul first of all, and check that it will comply with local regulations. Although certain developed countries may have a reasonable second-hand car market, you cannot always count on it.

Children of school age

If you are leaving your children in the UK with a relative or friend, you will need to leave contact addresses and make proper financial provision. If they are to attend a boarding school there is the matter of finding a suitable school. Some local education authorities have schools of this type and may be able to accommodate your offspring. If not, you will have to find a private establishment.

A number of agencies can advise you on suitable schools. The leading ones are:

● Gabbitas, Truman & Thring, 6-8 Sackville Street, Piccadilly, London W1X 2BR (tel: 01-734 1764).
● Independent Schools Information Service (ISIS), 56 Buckingham Gate, London SW1E 6AG (tel: 01-630 8793).

If you are taking them with you make sure there is some educational provision for them at your destination, and that there will be a place for them when they arrive. It is wise to check with your employer, the Embassy or the *ECIS Directory*.

If there is no suitable provision at all, correspondence tuition could be considered, and for advice on this you should approach World-wide Education Service, 44-50 Osnaburgh Street, London NW1 3NN (tel: 01-387 9228). Under the Service's Home School System, parents teach their own children with the guidance of WES tutors. The programme has been endorsed by the DES.

WES also provide an educational counselling service for employees with a number of British companies and agencies operating abroad.

Health

In some places the health facilities may be expensive or of a low standard, so make full use of NHS facilities before you leave, including

● a dental check
● a sight test
● a chest X-ray

Several employers insist that you have a medical check-up before you are confirmed in the post. Even if they do not, it may be wise to consult your GP as to your general state of fitness.

Your employer may provide health insurance while you are at post, or you may be expected to contribute to the state social security scheme, where it exists. However, it is worthwhile bearing in mind that in many countries state health care provision is much less extensive than in the UK.

The Department of Health publishes two free booklets — *SA40: Before you go* and *SA41: While you're away* — both of which deal with health matters abroad. If your local office does not have a copy, ring 0800 555777. If you will be travelling through an EC country you should also obtain form E111.

If you are travelling to Africa, parts of Latin America and Asia you will probably need to be vaccinated against cholera and possibly yellow fever and typhoid — particularly if you are likely to be living away from the main cities. You will also need to ensure you have a supply of anti-malarial pills and medicine to combat diarrhoea. Don't leave your vaccinations to the last moment.

Medical Advisory Services for Travellers Abroad Ltd (MASTA) can provide details of your vaccination and other medical requirements for a modest fee. (Contact them at the Bureau of Hygiene & Tropical Diseases, Keppel Street, London WC1E 7HT, tel: 01-636 8636). The Liverpool School of Tropical Medicine (tel: 051-708 9393) and the Hospital for Tropical Diseases (tel: 01-387 4411) can also advise.

Your GP will probably be able to vaccinate you, but you may find it more convenient to use the British Airways Vaccination Unit, 75 Regent Street, London W1R 7HG (tel: 01-439 9584) or a similar facility run by Thomas Cook at 45 Berkeley Square, London W1A 1EB (tel: 01-499 4000).

There are many good books on the market on how to keep healthy. If you don't have leanings towards hypochondria, the *Dictionary of Symptoms* by Dr Joan Gomez (Paladin) is a good buy and also *Travellers' Health* by Dr Richard Dawood (OUP). For anyone going to the tropics the Ross Institute (at the Bureau of Hygiene & Tropical Diseases address above) publishes a useful handbook called *Preservation of Personal Health in Warm Climates,* and there is also John Hatt's *The Tropical Traveller* (Pan).

Insurance

There are four types of insurance that you need to consider.

- Health and accident insurance — this is particularly vital if there is little social security provision in the country and your employer does not provide it.
- Personal effects insurance. Loss or damage to personal effects.
- Car insurance, if you happen to be taking a car.
- Life insurance, if you have dependants. The basic 'no frills' type is quite adequate.

For all of these it pays to consult a good broker who specialises in insurance for expatriates. Many advertise in the various expatriate magazines (see next page).

Investment

If you reckon that you are going to show a surplus on your earnings, it makes sense to look into ways in which you can invest your money:

Short-term investments

You need to have some reserves in ready cash in case of emergencies, and this means an investment account with a building society, bank or other reputable financial institution. Go for the account which offers a high rate of interest and withdrawal facilities on demand. If your salary is tax-free, go for an expatriate account where interest is paid free of tax. Banks in offshore tax havens, such as the Isle of Man and the Channel Islands, are well equipped to deal with this sort of thing, but your own bank or building society may well have the facilities you require.

Long-term investments

If you are likely to have cash that you will not need for a few years, it will probably be worth your while to invest it in equities. This is, of course, riskier — but the rewards are much greater, and this holds true the longer you keep your investment.

If surplus earnings are a relatively new phenomenon for you, tread carefully. Contact a few stockbrokers or investment advisers before you leave and describe your needs. Many will recommend unit trusts, investment trusts or a Personal Equity Plan (which has certain tax advantages) in order to spread the risk.

Investing in property, commodities, and individual companies is riskier for a beginner. The exception, of course, is buying your own home, but you need to make sure that it is fully insured and looked after in your absence.

The ins and outs of investment for expatriates are explained in *Working Abroad?* by Harry Brown (Northcote House) and a number of other handbooks. Magazines for expatriates will have useful investment articles as well as information on other matters relating to life overseas:

The Expatriate, 25 Brighton Road, South Croydon CR2 6EA

ExpatXtra, PO Box 300, Jersey, CI

Home and Away, 62 Tritton Road, London SE20 8DE

Resident Abroad, 102-108 Clerkenwell Rd, London WC1B 3PP

Luggage and personal effects

If you are travelling by air you won't be able to take everything with you unless your employer happens to be remarkably indulgent. Some luggage can be sent air-freight — which is much cheaper than the excess baggage rate — while the rest may have to be sent by sea or overland, which works out even cheaper.

To avoid undue worry and hassle contact a freight forwarding agent who can arrange for all aspects of transport from the packing stage onwards. If you are going to Europe and have a car, take as much luggage as possible with you.

Passport

Make certain that your passport is still valid and renew it, if necessary, through your local post office. If time is pressing, visit your regional Passport Office in person:

Greater London: Clive House, 70 Petty France, London SW1H 9HD

Scotland: 1st Floor, Empire House, 131 West Nile Street, Glasgow G1 2RY

Northern Ireland: Marlborough House, 30 Victoria Street, Belfast BT1 3LY

Northern England: 5th Floor, India Buildings, Water Street, Liverpool L2 0QZ

Wales and Western England: Olympia House, Upper Dock Street, Newport NP1 1XA

Midlands and Eastern England: 55 Westfield Road, Peterborough PE3 6TG

Pension

Is your job abroad pensionable? It probably isn't. In the case of some publicly funded posts you may receive a gratuity at the end of your term in lieu of a pension contribution, or you may be able to persuade your employer to contribute to your occupational pension.

As for your state pension at home, you can continue to make contributions on a voluntary basis. If you don't, you will not be eligible for the full entitlement when you retire. Since the state pension is index-linked, it makes good sense to keep up your payments.

If you haven't already done so, look into taking out a private pension scheme which you can continue when you return to the UK. Under current legislation you get tax relief if your pension contribution is 17½% or less of your total annual salary (more if you are over 50).

Certain employers may offer their own pension scheme, but this is rare. At the time of writing there are moves afoot to introduce a pension scheme for British Council contract staff.

Shopping

There are only three reasons for going on a big shopping spree before you leave, if you are to avoid a baggage problem:

● certain items are unavailable or in short supply in your adoptive country
● certain items are much more expensive there than at home
● certain items are going to be needed immediately upon arrival.

Try to find out about the availability and price of goods before you spend anything. Country profiles from Expatriate Briefings, the Women's Corona Society, the British Council, ODA, and some embassies will usually include such information.

If you are buying expensive items, you will probably be able to get them free of VAT provided you deal with a store which is au fait with the tax-free export scheme. Certain portable items — cameras, radios, cassette players — could be purchased en route at an airport duty-free shop.

A radio capable of receiving short-wave broadcasts is a must if you plan to keep in touch with what is happening back home.

Social Security

The DSS Overseas Branch, Newcastle-upon-Tyne NE98 1YX, publishes a series of booklets on all matters relating to social security, and it would be wise to write to them explaining where you are going and asking for advice. If you are heading for an EC country there is, for example, a series of guides entitled *Social Security for migrant workers*.

Your local DSS office may not have these leaflets, but should certainly be able to tell you what leaflets are available from the Overseas Branch.

Taxation

It is just as well to understand your tax liability both in the UK and abroad. Your employer or his agent ought to give you some idea on these matters, and you should not assume that similar organisations offer similar terms. British Council contract teachers, for instance usually get tax-free salaries, while those employed by the Overseas Development Administration do not.

You can obtain the information from a variety of sources:

- **The Inland Revenue** — either your local office or the Claims Branch, Foreign Division, Merton Road, Bootle L69 9BL. *Booklet IR25* sets out the rules governing the taxation of income from jobs overseas. The Inland Revenue publishes a number of leaflets, eg *The Taxation of Foreign Earnings and Pensions, Income Liable to UK Income Tax, Double Taxation Relief.*
- Handbooks, such as *Working Abroad?*
- Tax consultants
- Banks, particularly those in tax havens such as the Channel Islands.

If your tax affairs are complicated and there is a lot of money at stake, you could seek professional advice. Make sure that the consultant you engage is familiar with the tax problems of expatriates. Your bank may be able to advise you.

Travel

Most overseas employers will provide you with an economy class air ticket. Many will also provide tickets for your dependants. If there is some reluctance to do this ask for the fare equivalent in cash and contact a bucket shop or an agency like WEXAS which sells discounted fares.

Other modes of travel — by sea or overland — can be discounted, except in the case of Europe and perhaps North Africa, unless you have plenty of time at your disposal. In Europe sea and rail travel have much to commend them, since you can take much larger amounts of luggage with you.

If you have a car, car travel is another very sensible option within Europe and parts of the Middle East. Locations such as Turkey can be reached easily in a few days. But if your insurance policy is limited to the British Isles, inform your insurance company that you will need a 'green card' before you go.

Visas

Almost invariably you will need to obtain a visa if you are planning to work in a foreign country (the exceptions are the EC countries). To obtain a visa you will need to produce proof that you have a job offer and perhaps a statement from the authorities of the country concerned that the appointment has been approved.

Don't leave your visa application till the last minute. In some cases, the USA for example, it can take weeks or months for your application to be approved. This is less of a problem, however, in the case of exchange teaching schemes.

If you are travelling overland or plan to stop en route, check whether you will also need visas for the countries you pass through.

Miscellaneous points

- Will you need an international driving licence? Outside the European Community you probably will. Contact the AA or RAC for details.
- Make a will, just in case the unexpected happens — we are all mortal!
- Don't forget to make arrangements for the redirection of mail and make sure that your next of kin and other interested parties in the UK have an address for you.
- Get at least twelve passport photos of yourself and each member of your family travelling with you.
- Confirm arrival arrangements and ask for contact telephone numbers at your destination in case of emergency.
- If you are planning to travel extensively purchase a copy of *The Traveller's Handbook* (editor: Melissa Shales, Trade & Travel Publications). The reference section deals with such matters as visa requirements, customs offices, duty free allowances, airport departure taxes, currency restrictions, hospitals with English speaking staff, driving requirements worldwide, public holidays, business hours, freight forwarders, and so on. It also provides the addresses of foreign diplomatic representations and tourist boards in Australia, Canada, New Zealand and the USA as well as the UK, and also of the representations abroad of these countries.

PROFESSIONAL MATTERS

If you have very little time between appointment and departure you could be so preoccupied with the business of moving that you overlook the need for professional preparation. Yet if you are to get off to a good start professionally this shouldn't be skimped as there may be little opportunity for such preliminaries once you are on the job.

Preparation should not be confined to the subject(s) that you will be teaching. In order to be effective you need to have some understanding of the people you will be teaching, since their background — cultural and economic — may well affect their learning process and their attitudes towards education.

Culture

During your period of preparation remember that you will not just be teaching your subject, you will be teaching people. And it makes sense to learn just what makes them tick.

One of the most pleasurable ways of doing this is to read travel books or novels about the country. Go to a public library with an extensive travel section and browse. If you have something of a wanderlust, you might consider buying a guide book produced by Fodor, Baedeker or Lonely Planet, as well as a large scale map. In certain parts of the world good maps and guidebooks can be hard to come by.

Try to find out something about the history of the country both past and recent, since the past tends to shape attitudes and practices. You may not get a chance once you are in the country itself, since some of the more candid accounts could well be unavailable or banned.

Each nation has its own system of values: they may be different from your own but that doesn't mean they are inferior so it's important to understand these values. Learn to respect them, and perhaps to modify your own behaviour in deference to them, and you'll become more acceptable to your hosts, more at ease with your surroundings and more successful in your work. To start with, consider your own values. 'It is only by understanding his own origins and heritage that an individual can begin to make meaningful comparisons and truly enter into the world of receiving culture'. (David Wheatley, *Successful Expatriation — Bridging the Culture Gap,* published by Employment Conditions Abroad.)

Educational set-up

Familiarisation with the educational system and traditions of the country is important, even though you may be teaching in an organisation that stands outside the national educational system — an international school or a regional institute, for instance.

If you are teaching within the national system then you really should make an effort to understand it — how it has developed, what the government's educational policy is, how the education provision is structured, what subjects are taught and to whom, and so on. Without this knowledge some of the educational practices you come up against may strike you as bizarre or even irrational.

Above all, you need to understand something of the learning methods your students will be used to. In the Middle East, for instance, the old Koranic tradition of learning by rote is by no means extinct, and students can learn long passages by rote for reproduction during examinations, and yet not really understand what they have learned.

In other cultures too, knowledge is there to be assimilated, never applied. Students regard the teacher as a fount of wisdom, whose ideas should never be contradicted. The idea of thinking for oneself is alien to them, perhaps because their society favours conformism rather than originality.

The teacher's position needs to be understood, too. For example, is he or she a person who is respected or merely taken for granted? In many countries educational institutions and their teachers enjoy much less autonomy than they do in the UK. The ground rules are laid down by a centralist ministry and you are expected to adhere to these. As a consequence, your principal may turn out to be less of a decision-maker and professional leader than one might expect in Anglo-Saxon countries. Instead, he is largely an administrator with the unenviable task of ensuring that government directives are complied with.

Some educational systems are highly selective and elitist; others subscribe to the comprehensive ideal. Some have a strongly clerical atmosphere; others are decidedly anti-clerical. The educational traditions of a country often have a strong bearing on what happens in its schools and colleges, and concepts which may seem strange to a newcomer can sometimes only be explained by reference to the past.

Useful reference books are:

● *International Handbook of Education Systems,* John Wiley & Sons (in three volumes)
● *The UNESCO Statistical Yearbook*

Then there are books on individual countries and regions, and here the best idea is to browse through the comparative education section of a university or college of education library. Certain embassies (or their cultural centres) may be able to provide booklets on education in their countries, and there are surveys on various educational systems by the Council of Europe, OECD, UNESCO and Britain's DES.

The following series may well have a title dealing with the country you are planning to teach in:

● *World Education Series,* David & Charles
● *Society, Schools and Progress Series,* Pergamon
● *Reviews of National Policies for Education,* OECD
● *English Teaching Profiles,* British Council English Teaching Information Centre
● The *World Education Series* of the American Association of Collegiate Registrars and Admissions Officers

More books on specific regions and countries are listed in the **Further Reading** appendix. Education in many countries has changed very rapidly in the last decade or so, and it is important to consult books that are up-to-date, as well as recent issues of journals such as the *Comparative Education*.

Language

If you are going to a country where English is not the mother-tongue, you may find it frustrating that so few people understand you. It will be helpful to have at least a smattering of the language on arrival, and there are many methods available for learning the rudiments of a language:

- **Language learning manuals.** The Teach Yourself Books are the best known series and have the advantage of being widely available. An academic bookshop which has an extensive language section, such as Foyles, Dillons, Blackwells or Collets, will show what else is on offer.

- **Audio courses.** The emphasis here is on the spoken language, which is going to be of immense importance to you. The following organisations distribute and/or publish courses of this nature:
  Linguaphone, 124-126 Brompton Road, Knightsbridge, London SW3
  Audio Forum, 31 Kensington Church Street, London W8 4LL (tel: 01-937 1647)
  BBC Publications, 35 Marylebone High Street, London W1M 4AA

- **Part-time courses.** Many local colleges provide part-time courses in the more common languages, and in London and other large centres the range of languages taught can be quite considerable. Certain universities and polytechnics have their own language centres which offer facilities for casual students. Some countries, like France and W. Germany, have their own cultural institutes which offer language tuition, and there are many private language schools which offer courses as well. Consult your local *Yellow Pages* for details of the nearest.

- **Intensive courses.** If your departure is imminent there is a lot to be said for learning as much as you can in the short time available. Some universities, polytechnics and local colleges run intensive courses. Otherwise there are private sector colleges which specialise in this type of course. Notable ones are:
  Berlitz, 79 Wells Street, 321 Oxford Street, London W1A 3BZ
  Inlingua, 50 Fitzroy Street, London W1P 5HS

- **Private Tuition.** Many colleges can put you in touch with private tutors. Private schools, like those mentioned above, will often be prepared to provide one-to-one tuition for you.

The Centre for Information on Language Teaching and Research publishes *Language and Culture Guides* which contain information on courses in less commonly taught languages and a leaflet entitled *Part-time and Intensive Language Study*. Address: Regent's College, Inner Circle, Regent's Park, London NW1 4NS (tel: 01-468 8221).

Your own subject

When you arrive at your posting you will be expected not only to be knowledgeable in your subject but also to be able to adapt that knowledge to the local environment. For example, if you are an economist going to teach in the Third World some knowledge of development economics will be useful.

Some form of preparation is vital, but in order to avoid wasting time on what will prove to be irrelevant, you need to ask for guidance. Try to track down your predecessor in the job or someone who has worked in the area before, and question them in detail along the following lines:

- What are educational standards like?
- What does the syllabus consist of and what textbooks are used?
- What books/equipment/materials do you suggest I take?
- To what extent is it possible to produce my own teaching materials (ie are there photocopiers, duplicators, typewriters, word processors, an adequate supply of paper in the school/college)?
- What are library and bookshop facilities like?
- What facilities are there for research?
- What facilities are there for practical work (laboratories, computers, tape recorders, etc)?
- Are there any locally produced studies in my subject of which I ought to be aware?
- Are there any induction courses available?
- What type of professional support can I expect (advisers, teachers' centres, etc)?

The choice of which books to take can be a problem. If you have an extensive library of your own, resign yourself to the thought that you'll have to leave most of it behind. Not even the most generous baggage allowance will allow you to ship hundreds of treasured volumes. You'll have to be selective, and again some kind of guidance will be needed on which volumes to take. If you are going to a country which has a rich assortment of libraries, the dilemma may not be so acute.

If there is some doubt as to how easy it is to obtain books at your new posting, it may well be worthwhile to open an account with an academic bookseller who offers a reliable mail order service.

5
The Cultural Challenge

SETTLING IN

No matter how well you have prepared yourself for the experience of living and working in a foreign environment, you will not be able to judge whether you have made the right decision until you actually arrive. Even then, first impressions may not be the correct ones, since it takes time to settle in.

The sort of person who is enthusiastic about his new location right from the start may find that the novelty begins to pall after a time. Another type may find the first few days or weeks the most anxious of his life and come to the speedy conclusion that he has made a terrible mistake. Yet after a time he begins to appreciate both his new home and his job.

The initial period is an absolutely crucial time when you have to be at your most alert. For in addition to coming to grips with new professional challenges you are also involved in making suitable domestic arrangements for yourself in unfamiliar surroundings.

This section touches on some of the problems that you may encounter at first and suggests ways in which you might cope with them.

YOUR ARRIVAL

Your arrival at a strange airport (or station or port) after a long journey can be a bewildering experience when a helping hand can be very useful. With luck there will be someone there to meet you and put you right, but don't count on it.

It is sensible to prepare yourself in advance in case of misadventure:

- Arm yourself with one or two contact addresses or telephone numbers.
- Try to have some local currency by you in case the *bureaux de change* are shut.

- Carry a decent guide book with you which lists accommodation addresses.

You may have to deal with immigration and customs yourself. This is a fairly simple procedure in most of Europe, but in other areas of the world it can be a wearisome and time-consuming experience. You may be required to show a letter from your employer, for example, and fill in copious forms.

When all is completed, if you look at the stamp that has been put in your passport and find that it is valid for only seven days, don't despair. You will probably need to register within this period in order to obtain your residence permit.

If someone has come to meet you and you have doubts about your documentation, check with him that you have acted correctly before you leave your port of arrival. If, on the other hand, the expected welcoming party has failed to materialise, again don't despair.

- Check with the information desk for any messages
- Telephone one of your contacts.
- Mention your problem to a representative of the airline you have arrived by.
- If everything else fails, leave a message and look round for an accommodation booking service and transport into town.

ACCOMMODATION

Short-term

It is quite usual for new teachers to spend their initial period in a hotel, and this is a sensible idea. The first 24 hours need to be a period of acclimatisation when you sleep off the journey, if it has been a lengthy one, and are free of domestic concerns.

After a time the novelty of living in a hotel begins to wear off, particularly if you have a family. As quickly as possible you need to find a place of residence for the long-term. You won't feel truly at home and able to concentrate fully on your professional duties until you have taken this step.

Hotel accommodation, in any case, can work out expensive, and it is advisable to check with your employer, if you have not already done so, what elements — if any — you have to pay for. The initial period is likely to be an expensive time anyway, and you don't want to have to spend vast amounts of cash on hotel bills.

In some cases, however, new arrivals are put into permanent accommodation right away.

Long-term

Comfortable accommodation can play an important part in making your life palatable. Teaching abroad is not without its frustrations and you need to be able to escape from it all at the end of the day in order to relax. The question is: can you?

Accommodation arrangements differ and this should have been made clear to you before you signed the contract. The employing institution may provide accommodation for you; it may give you a rent allowance; or alternatively — and this is particularly the case within Europe — paying for accommodation may be your own responsibility entirely.

Accommodation **provided by the employer** can be first class or downright mediocre. Before you signed the contract you should have been given some indication as to what to expect, but the moment of truth does not come until you arrive.

For teachers accommodated in a boarding establishment there may be disadvantages which you failed to anticipate. Instead of being able to escape from your duties at the end of each day, you may find that you are permanently on call or surrounded by the noise of children from early in the morning till late at night. If it is in an isolated location you may find your social horizon is excessively limited.

It is as well to recall that in signing the contract you signify your agreement to certain conditions. If the accommodation differs considerably from what you were led to believe at your interview or briefing, you have grounds for complaint. If it does not, you really have to accept it.

Generally speaking, teachers feel happier if they can **find their own accommodation.** Yet this can present problems, particularly when rented accommodation is scarce. In a sense, you have enough on your plate coming to grips with your new job, and trailing around to find suitable accommodation can be a chore.

Don't be afraid to seek advice. Find out which areas expatriates prefer — where the transport and shopping are good, for instance. While you may have a fairly good idea of the kind of accommodation you would like, remember that an old hand will have useful knowledge about matters that are less apparent to the newcomer. Some areas may be prone to flooding, power cuts and water shortages. In others security may be a problem.

If you have been recruited by an organisation such as the British Council or an international company, the local office staff should be able to put you right and render you invaluable assistance. If you are dealing with an organisation with little experience of coping with expatriates, you may not be quite so lucky.

Teachers recruited in Europe will often be expected to find and finance their own accommodation. This may not present a problem if there is plenty available, but in university towns especially there is a high demand from students for low-cost rented accommodation. You may find that you have to pay a premium on the rent — up to a year in advance — or you could be presented with a formidable looking legal document to sign.

One way to overcome such obstacles is to confront your employers with the problem and find out if they can help. They may be able to offer the landlord certain guarantees or negotiate a better deal. If you can persuade them to sign the contract and deduct the rent from your salary, so much the better. Organisations tend to have more clout than individuals.

If you are a student teacher (assistant) in a university town you may be able to use the accommodation bureau of the university. Newspapers and private accommodation bureaux are other sources of accommodation addresses. However, some of the best value accommodation is found by word of mouth, so it pays to ask around.

YOUR FIRST PROFESSIONAL CONTACTS

One of the first things you will need to do is establish contact with your workplace. First meetings can be crucial and your aim must be to make a favourable impression on everybody. So it is sensible to dress smartly for the occasion, unless advised otherwise.

Women have to be particularly scrupulous about dress. In Muslim countries, in particular, long dresses and covered shoulders are *de rigeur* — and trousers could cause offence in places. In educational establishments it is best to dress decorously — which can mean drably, I'm afraid — so you will have to save your natty outfits for social occasions.

If you are not certain what to wear, ask for advice. You may find, to your relief, that Savile Row elegance is not expected of you. Informal attire is more likely to be accepted in expatriate-run language schools than in more formal educational establishments.

Ideally the first encounter should be limited to meeting people and having a quick look round. If there are any pressing problems, such as accommodation, by all means bring them up, but it is wise to leave the nitty gritty till later.

Not every first encounter is necessarily an ideal one, unfortunately. Term may have started, and you could find yourself being pushed into a classroom within minutes of your arrival! You may find your colleagues so rushed off their feet that a lengthy briefing is just out of the question.

Even if you arrive in advance of the start of term, you cannot assume that you will be put fully into the picture. Not all heads of departments or principals are particularly good at briefing people. They just take it for granted that everybody knows the intricacies of their establishment. Be prepared for this by compiling in advance a list of questions you will need to ask.

Suggested questions

In general, you will need to know:

- Who is who in the establishment and to whom am I responsible?
- What precisely are my duties?
- Will I have extra duties apart from teaching?
- What are the working hours?

More specifically:

- What is the syllabus?
- How much discretion do I have in teaching methods and materials?
- Am I expected to produce detailed lesson plans for inspection?
- Is there a register in which I have to record attendance and/or the content of my lessons?
- What teaching facilities does the school/college have, apart from blackboards and classrooms, and how do I book them?

About your students:

- What is the background of my students?
- How motivated are they?
- What disciplinary problems arise and how are they dealt with?
- How are students assessed?

● Which marking schemes are used and how should marks be recorded?

Concerning your financial position:

● When are salaries paid?
● What, if any, deductions are made?
● Is it possible to get an advance if I need one?

If there are **expatriate staff** in the establishment they will probably be able to tell you what you need to know without too much prodding. Beware, however, of taking every remark at its face value. Some 'old hands' may have a tendency to mix opinion with facts, and it is the facts that you are after at this stage, not other people's prejudices.

On the other hand you may be the only expatriate on the staff, and may find you have to probe for answers. Don't bombard your colleagues with too many questions as they may find this intimidating. Try instead to extract information from them by degrees. Some of this can be learned by example. See if you can sit in on lessons to find how other teachers handle their classes.

SORTING OUT PROBLEMS

Not every landing proves to be a happy one. The institution and the job may fall far short of your expectations. There may be some kind of confusion as to your role. Perhaps your accommodation is not up to standard, or certain conditions relating to your contract are not being fulfilled. You may even find that you are superfluous to staffing requirements or that no-one knows what to do with you.

There are three options open to you:

● You can walk out.
● You can complain.
● You can shrug your shoulders and decide to make the best of a bad job.

Walking out can prove costly. Not that you will necessarily be sued for breach of contract, but you may have to pay your fare home and find yourself out of work for a while. However, if after careful consideration you feel that you have been placed in an impossible situation which is unlikely to improve, retreat may be the best solution.

Complaining can be more fruitful, if you find the right person. The obvious people to turn to are the organisation that recruited you. This should present no problem if they happen to have a local representative.

Even if they don't, I think it is important to put the onus on them to solve any misunderstanding rather than wade into the fray yourself. Only do this when all other approaches fail.

The third alternative, **to grin and bear it,** may be the wisest move in the long run. If your employers recognise that you have been lured to their establishment under false pretences, they may be prepared to go some way to meeting your demands. This will not happen, however, if you go round making mountains out of molehills or asking for things which are not specified in the contract.

ESTABLISHING A RELATIONSHIP

Bear in mind that during this initial period you are, in effect, establishing a bridgehead. Once you have a secure and comfortable base you will be able to concentrate on the important task of establishing a good relationship with your colleagues, superiors, and ultimately, your students.

GETTING DOWN TO WORK

The first days or weeks in a new environment often have something of the character of a holiday. It is a stimulating period much enjoyed by people who revel in novel experiences, and something of a shock for people who acclimatise more slowly.

This period does not last. The novelty begins to wear off, and you settle into a routine. Teachers in the first category may discover that the place where they have landed is not as attractive as they thought at first, while the slow adapters gradually come to terms with it, and may even come to like it. But it is only now that you discover whether you have made the right decision or not.

This section points out potential problems. Not that you will necessarily encounter more than a few. However, it is just as well to be aware of what could happen in order to avoid trouble.

RELATIONSHIPS

With colleagues

You could find yourself in a tightly-knit expatriate community where everyone lives virtually on top of each other, perhaps on the same campus. On the other hand you might be the only foreigner on the staff and find yourself practically ignored.

In the first situation you will certainly not lack for professional advice. In fact, you could get smothered by it. In the latter case you may not get any advice at all, so it is important to establish at least a professional relationship. Try to pin someone down, preferably your head of department if you have one, and ask for direction. It is a mistake to concentrate solely on doing your own thing.

Unless it happens to be part of your brief, don't cast yourself as a new broom that has come to sweep clean, otherwise you could cause resentment. After all, your colleagues have a headstart on you as they are already familiar with the teaching situation. Admittedly not all will be as well qualified as you may be, and as a result may nurse an inferiority complex. This could manifest itself in downright opposition to any proposals you make designed to improve teaching. You need to recognise that change can only come about gradually and with the approval of all concerned.

With students
Your relationship with your students will vary according to their age and cultural background. Many of the younger ones in the state system will be used to quite formal teaching methods, and may act disruptively if you adopt a more relaxed approach in the classroom. In parts of the Third World rote learning is still very much entrenched. Ask if you can observe a few lessons to see how other teachers handle their classes.

Generally speaking, students like teachers they can respect, not someone who panders to them. It is a wise policy not to cultivate familiarity — in the early stages, at least — unless you are dealing with mature students.

With other expatriates
There is no need to go completely native. Cultivate the friendship of other expatriates, by all means. A lot of them will be more comfortably off than you are, particularly if they are in business or the diplomatic service. Nevertheless you probably have a lot to offer them. If you are in an international school, for example, you could be teaching their children.

Aim for a lifestyle that is congenial rather than extravagant, and avoid becoming a member of an inward-looking clique who do nothing but bemoan the customs of the natives — even if the natives do happen to be fellow-Europeans!

With local people
'When in Rome do as the Romans do.' This is a useful adage, but should not be taken to extremes, particularly if you find yourself living in an obscure village in a remote Third World country. Indeed, the locals could find it offensive if you try to ape them in every way.

Most nationals have a concept of how a British person behaves. It may be an old-fashioned concept fashioned by P.G. Wodehouse novels, but it is on the whole positive. If you deviate too much from the conceived norm, people will be puzzled and even outraged. There is no need to cultivate the image of the stiff upper lip, but you will need to exercise discretion in your behaviour and your relationships. In a sense you are an ambassador for your own country, and you set the standard by which your fellow-countrymen will be judged!

LOCAL ATTITUDES & CUSTOMS

Your relationships with local people will be much enhanced if you take pains to understand and respect their local customs. Even in societies which you believe to be similar to your own there can be surprisingly different attitudes. Here are a few matters where circumspection may be necessary.

Politics

Avoid political discussions except with people that you have come to know very well. While people may feel free to criticise their own government quite mercilessly, they may resent a foreigner doing so. In less secure countries criticism of the government by a foreigner could land you in jail.

Religion

Religious practices in certain countries may seem bizarre but religion is a sensitive issue, and you must learn to live with it. Be careful about discussing your own religious beliefs in case you are suspected of proselytising. (If you are a teacher in a missionary school this advice may not apply!)

Girl meets boy

Many societies adopt very protective attitudes towards their women, and arranged marriages are often the norm. For a foreign male even to invite a girl out to dinner unchaperoned could provoke a scandal in some countries. Women teachers have to be particularly circumspect in male dominated societies, as friendly interest can easily be misinterpreted. Make sure you are aware of local attitudes before you enter into any close relationship with someone of the opposite sex.

The law

Foreigners are not above the law, and have no special rights and privileges. Therefore, it is important not to flout the law of the land, even if you feel that certain aspects of it are nonsensical (for example, a ban on the consumption of alcohol). In some countries sentences can be severe — drug trafficking offences may incur the death penalty, working illegally without a work permit could well lead to instant deportation. Ignorance of the local laws is no defence in the courts.

PROFESSIONAL PROBLEMS

Textbooks

You may well find that the textbooks issued to students are inappropriate, biased or just plain hopeless. However, if you try to change them right at the outset you could cause an uproar. In schools, particularly, you may find that books are prescribed by the Ministry of Education and cannot be changed. Or there may be a problem in getting new supplies. Try to make the best of a bad job — for the time being, at least. Inspired teaching, however, can compensate for a great deal, even an inadequate textbook.

A more serious problem arises when there are no textbooks at all. This is a common occurrence in Third World countries which are short of foreign exchange, and it can also happen in the most exclusive schools and colleges in the most developed of countries where orders have gone astray.

Facilities

If you have worked in a well-equipped establishment with videos, photocopiers, overhead projectors, visual aids and so on, you could be in for a shock. Chalk and a blackboard in every room may be the sum total of facilities in your educational establishment. The notion of specially prepared worksheets done on duplicators or photocopiers may have to be given a miss.

A situation like this can be particularly frustrating for a teacher of science or practical subjects. Students may have no opportunity to learn by doing, but instead have to rely exclusively on textbooks.

On the other hand you may be in an establishment where equipment is locked away and never used, or just doesn't work. In cases like this, make a few discreet enquiries and offer to show your colleagues how these items can be used. If you demonstrate tremendous zeal, you may even end up in charge of all the teaching aids.

Syllabus

In many countries the syllabus for schools, and sometimes even for universities, is laid down by the government. Education inspectors will come round occasionally to check not on the quality of the teaching but on whether teachers are adhering to the syllabus.

The syllabus may be unbelievably bad, but you will have to cope with it as best you can. In the long-term, however, you may be able to influence future policy. Schools or professional bodies sometimes have the right to make recommendations to the Ministry regarding possible changes.

Standards
Educational standards vary from country to country and often within countries. You may be pleasantly surprised; on the other hand you could be appalled — especially at the tertiary level, when you compare the amount of knowledge you had to acquire to gain your own first degree with the abysmal standards your students have to attain.

There is no easy solution to this problem. If you try to raise standards, students complain that the exams are too difficult. If you don't, you are really deluding people into thinking they are more competent than they probably are. The moment of truth comes when they apply to do a postgraduate course at a foreign university.

Irregularities
In some countries a diploma is worth its weight in gold, and people will stop at nothing in order to gain one. One matter that you may have to come to terms with is cheating — or 'co-operation' — in examinations and written assignments.

You could also find that some of your poorly-paid colleagues are accepting inducements to pass students, or that pressure is put on you to upgrade the marks of students that you consider hopeless, particularly if they come from influential families.

Red tape
Most educational systems, particularly highly centralised ones, have their share of red tape. Permission may have to be applied for to leave the country for a short holiday; minutes of staff meetings have to be read and signed; you may be confronted with a plethora of forms; and towards the end of the academic year when marks have to be totted up and examinations held, things can get even worse.

In most cases there is little you can do, since these procedures are laid down by law. So don't make a fuss, but try to understand them and comply with them. Your colleagues probably detest the administrative details every bit as much as you.

HEALTH
You will not be able to cope with all the rigours of your professional duties unless you are in the peak of condtion, so maintenance of good

health is a top priority. This doesn't mean you should become a hypochondriac. You just need to take sensible precautions and act swiftly if your condition deteriorates.

Physical health

The aim must be prevention, and in tropical areas this means avoiding tap water and uncooked vegetables, taking prescribed prophylactics, as well as deterring disease carrying insects. (The Ross Institute Health booklet gives some very useful tips — see p.61.)

Exercise ought to form part of your daily routine, whether it be sport or a less strenuous activity such as walking.

If you fall ill, don't put off a visit to a physician. He is much more familiar with local diseases and ailments than you are, and will normally be able to prescribe a speedy cure.

Mental health

In a strange environment there is always a minority who find that they are unable to cope. All of us feel depressed at one time or another, and the problem can be accentuated if you find yourself in strange surroundings.

Depression may spring from homesickness, a feeling of isolation, overwork, an inability to come to terms with your surroundings, social pressures, and so on. It is often associated with alcoholism and may lead to a breakdown of some kind.

There are various ways to avoid drifting into a state of acute depression:

- Keep your brain active. Read, study, learn the local language, write your memoirs!
- Keep in touch with home through letters, magazines and newspapers, short wave radio broadcasts.
- Get away for weekends and short holidays as often as possible.
- Meet people. If you are not far from a large expatriate community, join a club, go to the local church.
- If everything else fails consult a doctor who will probably prescribe anti-depressant drugs.
- Don't hit the bottle! Excessive alcohol consumption could make you even worse.

PREMATURE TERMINATION OF CONTRACT

In principle, contracts are meant to be kept rather than broken, and you should endeavour to complete yours unless you have good reasons not to do so. This is important not only from the point of view of your employer but also from that of your future. When you apply for posts in the future, a prospective employer may have second thoughts about taking you on if he sees that you have walked out on a job.

You therefore need to weigh up the pros and cons very carefully to make sure you have good reasons to quit. Otherwise, try to see your contract out.

The following are justifiable reasons for leaving the post prematurely:

- Ill-health
- Domestic problems
- Fundamental disagreement with your employer
- Failure by the employer to honour the terms of your contract
- Problems with the job that will never be resolved (this may be a tricky one).

Wherever possible ensure that the contract is terminated by mutual agreement, and that you and your employers and/or superiors part on good terms. After all, you may need to approach them for a reference in the future.

6
The Next Step

When you read this chapter you may have a sense of *déjà vu*. It may remind you of where you came in at the first chapter. The last six months of your contract are a time for making decisions. Indeed, you may find yourself pressed by your employers to make up your mind even sooner as to whether you intend to renew your contract.

Decisions, decisions! If you are back home, you do not have to go through this exercise so frequently. However, since virtually all teaching positions abroad tend to be fixed contract posts, every one, two or three years the teacher has to consider his future. Even if you enjoy the rare privilege of security of tenure, it is wise to **review your options** periodically.

YOUR OPTIONS

Renewal of contract

The end of your contract need not necessarily betoken upheaval. In many instances contracts can be renewed. Indeed, if you have acquitted yourself well at your place of work, superiors and colleagues will no doubt encourage you to stay on.

But, given the uncertain nature of an overseas teaching career, is this the best option? If you are content with your work and your circumstances, you may well feel that it is. After all, at home teachers and lecturers stay in the same job for years — even right up to retirement. Not everyone considers it beneficial to chop and change.

On the other hand, staying on might be regarded as an easy way out. You are postponing your decision until the next time your contract comes up for renewal, and the longer you stay in the place the more difficult it is to uproot yourself and move elsewhere.

The financial factor should not be disregarded. Generally speaking, if you agree to renew, you should be offered a carrot in the shape of **increased remuneration.** On the other hand, you could find yourself worse off if your hitherto tax-free salary becomes liable to income tax, as is the case, for example, in Sweden when the initial two years are up.

Finding another job in the same country

If you feel very much at home in your adoptive country, and really don't want to leave, you could consider taking up another job. If there is a **prestigious opportunity** going, by all means apply, even if it stipulates higher qualifications than you possess.

Remember that by dint of your experience you will be a strong contender for the post, particularly against an outsider however well qualified.

Don't change for the sake of change however, since it may cause resentment among your current colleagues and employers.

Finding another job abroad

Should you opt to move on, it is wise to get cracking at an early stage — certainly six months or so before the termination date of your contract.

The first people to inform and consult are those at the agency that recruited you. If they are happy with you and you are with them, ask them to keep you in mind for another post and state your preferences.

If you have home leave it makes sense to visit a number of different recruitment agencies to let them see your face, and to find out the lie of the jobs market.

Some organisations issue vacancy bulletins, notably the **British Council, Christians Abroad** and **International House.** Ask to be put on the mailing lists of those that do. Otherwise spend time browsing through the job advertisement columns of the appropriate newspapers. Most British Council libraries, for instance, take the Times educational supplements.

If you have colleagues in other countries in the same line of business, contact them to see if they know of any openings.

In the early stages of your quest make up your mind that you want to move forward. Try for a job with more responsibility than the one you have at present. Alternatively, consider moving sideways into a field that is connected with your present work but not exactly the same — **teacher training,** for example.

Finding another job at home

This may be trickier. For one thing you are less accessible when it comes to interviews, and most home institutions are not prepared to consider you unless they have had a chance to see you face to face. Moreover, you may have to pay your own travel expenses.

In the case of Overseas Development Administration and British Council appointees there is an **Interview Fund** which pays a proportion of your travel expenses if you need to return to the UK for an interview for a senior post. Not everyone is eligible, however, and applications have to be submitted in advance of the date of travel. (Write to: Room E347, ODA, Eland House, Stag Place, London SW1E 5DH; Committee for International Co-operation in Higher Education, British Council, 10 Spring Gardens, London SW1A 2BN.)

In addition to keeping your eyes glued to recruitment advertisements, send **speculative letters** to local authorities, schools and colleges in both the state and the public sector to find out if they know of any vacancies. Contact recruitment agencies, such as Gabbitas, Truman & Thring, which recruit for UK schools as well as overseas ones. It might be sensible to contact **your union** as well.

If you have not managed to fix up a job before you return to Britain, there is no need to despair. You can resort to stop-gap measures.

- **A temporary job.** This is particularly easy in the summer when language schools all over Britain require staff in the form of teachers, social organisers and course leaders. Don't overlook opportunities in tourism and related industries.
- **Supply teaching.** Either register with the education authority in the area in which you normally live and offer your services, or try one of the big metropolitan education authorities which are constantly on the lookout for supply staff.

Enrolling for a course

Absence from home for a considerable number of years may mean that you are out of touch with the latest developments in your field, in which case a period of study might be appropriate. The DES arrange a number of short **refresher courses** under the direction of HM inspectors lasting between three and fourteen days. Longer courses, both full-time and part-time, are dealt with in the DES handbook *Long Courses for Teachers*. The Teachers' Branch of the DES can provide further information.

There are certain factors which may act as a deterrent to taking a course.

Lack of finance?

While some teachers arrive home with their finances in a very healthy state, this is not true of everybody, and you may think twice about spending all your assets on a course of study. Moreover, you are probably not eligible for a local authority grant, even a discretionary one, having just returned from abroad. Don't be deterred from trying though, and also investigate other sources of finance (see *The Grants Register* published by Macmillan).

The ODA operates the **Educational Development Scheme** which offers a small number of awards to anyone wishing to continue working in the Third World. The deadline for applications is normally March (Room AH 372). For young English teachers there is a **Postgraduate Training Award Scheme** (Room AH 364) particularly suited to volunteers.

Don't overlook the training grants on offer from the Government's Training Agency. These are for approved vocationally-oriented courses in technology, management, computers, etc, of up to one year. Even if you want to embark on a course of study which is not approved, the Agency may approve it if you put up a good enough case.

Too late to register?
While you often have to register for an undergraduate course up to nine months in advance, this is not the case with all postgraduate or training courses. Decide which course you would like to do and contact a number of the establishments which offer it, explaining your position.

Too old to learn?
This is a nonsense. We live in the age of the mature student. Middle-aged people are returning to study in increasing numbers these days. They have to, in order to keep abreast of modern developments. You'll need to brush up your study skills, of course, and the first month may be traumatic getting back in the old routine. But the stimulus should prove well worthwhile.

Unwilling to commit yourself to full-time study?
The number of opportunities for part-time study is increasing. Many tertiary institutions offer part-time study courses, notably Birkbeck College of London University. You can also study by correspondence with the Open University, the Open College, and several other institutions for all manner of degrees and certificates including external degrees of London University.

Changing direction and getting advice
It may be that you want to strike out into new territory or are uncertain which direction your career should follow. One way of resolving the dilemma is to talk things over with your superiors or colleagues and listen to their views. VSO and SCEA are two organisations that offer advice and assistance to their returnees. Most others don't. In such a situation you could turn to one of the following organisations for advice:

- Christians Abroad, 11 Carteret Street, London SW1H 9DL
- The Department of Employment (Job Centre). Since the PER was privatised in October 1988 and stopped operating their useful half-day job-hunting seminars, the main source of advice on public sector counselling is now your local Job Centre.
- the careers counselling unit of your old university or college. Some local colleges offer a similar service, as do some LEA careers offices
- independent careers counsellors.

Many of the larger independents such as Connaught, Interexec, Chusid Lander, and the Vocational Guidance Association (now a private company), advertise nationally. Smaller, more localised outfits can be found in the *Yellow Pages*.

The cost of private counselling can range from £150 to a few thousand pounds. The different fees charged indicate the level of service offered. A basic service will usually consist of an aptitude and personality test followed by a counselling session and/or written report. An intermediate service will offer the basic service plus counselling sessions, help with interview techniques, CV preparation, and so on, until you land a new job. A full service will be the intermediate service plus an extensive marketing campaign, mounted by the organisation, and temporary assignments.

The following organisations offer basic guidance to individuals at fees starting at around £200 or less:

- Career Analysts, 90 Gloucester Place, London W1H 4BL (tel: 01-935 5452)
- Career Assessment Services, Melbourne House, Melbourne Street, Brighton BN2 3LH (tel: 0273 675299)
- Careers Advisory & Business Services, 18 Winchcombe Street, Cheltenham GL52 2LX (tel: 0242 224616)
- Independent Assessment & Research Centre, 57 Marylebone High Street, London W1M 3AE (tel: 01-935 2373)
- Mid-Career Development Centre, 77 Morland Road, Croydon CR0 6EA (tel: 01-654 0808)
- Vocational Guidance Association, 7 Harley House, Upper Harley Street, London NW1 4RP (tel: 01-935 2600).

Teaching abroad in the long term

Is it possible to spend one's whole career abroad? That very much depends on the nature and location of your job. Very few posts apart from those in the missionary field are to be seen as long-term engagements.

In some developed countries security of **tenure** is possible in an educational institution, particularly at the tertiary level. This is not generally the case, though, in the Third World, where governments hope eventually to replace expensive expatriate teachers and lecturers by their own nationals. Another possibility, if you are prepared to take on more of an **administrative role,** is to find a permanent post with an educational organisation with outlets in foreign countries, such as the British Council or a language school group.

The majority of teaching posts abroad, however, tend to be **contract based,** and however permanent your prospects look, remember that unforeseen events such as war, an economic downturn or revolution could put an end to your dreams of permanence. You therefore cannot afford to rest on your laurels. You need to keep up with the latest developments in your field and treat yourself to the occasional refresher course in order to remain a marketable proposition. Otherwise you may find yourself at a disadvantage when you are obliged to move on to another post, and returning to work in your chosen field in the British Isles could prove very difficult.

A bright future ahead

Throughout this book I have tended to focus on the perils of venturing abroad as a teacher or lecturer and understate the advantages. My motive has not been to discourage you from taking such a step but rather to prepare you for the type of eventuality you might have to face.

But let me end on a positive note.

To start with, the chances are that you will need to face up to only a fraction of the problems detailed in this book. Indeed, many teachers and lecturers enjoy trouble-free contracts during which they encounter fewer hassles than they would at home. Secondly, teaching abroad can be immensely stimulating if you approach it in the right frame of mind. An overseas posting can open up marvellous opportunities to travel and get to know people. It is an experience that few regret and many cherish. Thirdly, provided you are suitably qualified, there will continue to be a ready market for your skills. Education is an expanding business, and there are opportunities galore for people of all ages who are prepared to look for them.

Education is also an international business, and I foresee a much freer flow of teachers between countries in the next decade. After 1992, for example, people will be able to pursue their profession in any country of the European Community without the need to requalify.

For teachers wanting to return to the UK the prospects look better than they have for a decade. Demographic trends mean that Britain is facing a shortage of trained people, particularly at the younger end of the scale. After a downturn in teaching posts, teachers are now in short supply, particularly in such subjects as languages, commercial subjects, science and mathematics. Another consideration is that the jobs market in Britain is more fluid these days, so changing direction has become much easier.

Finally your cosmopolitan outlook and experience of other countries and cultures could prove a considerable asset to a firm or organisation that is having to think internationally — perhaps for the first time.

In short, prospects have never looked brighter for teachers and lecturers wishing either to work abroad or to return to Britain. Develop awareness of your abilities and potential and of the many opportunities available, and you can look to the future with optimism.

7
The Teaching Scene Worldwide

REGIONS OF THE WORLD

Africa

The problem with many countries in Africa is that they are short of teachers and short of cash, **South Africa** being the main exception. Although most aspire to the goal of universal education, it is often something of an achievement if 50% of children in a particular country receive a primary education. Secondary education is the privilege of a much smaller percentage.

In many African schools classes are large, with a ratio in excess of 50 pupils per teacher in many cases. The best educational provision tends to be in the towns and cities. Facilities in the rural areas are poor, and illiteracy rates are correspondingly high. Civil war, famine, low commodity prices or mismanagement compound the problems in certain countries.

Yet it is not all gloom and doom. Resource-rich countries with small populations, such as **Gabon** and **Botswana,** have been able to invest in schools and colleges. In parts of French-speaking Africa there are innovative schemes designed to improve education in rural areas and attempts to tailor the school curriculum more precisely to the needs of the country. International agencies such as the World Bank and UNDP are particularly active in this field, and so are a number of voluntary agencies.

Africa is by no means a homogeneous continent. Its destiny over the past century has been shaped by the colonial powers that have imposed their own languages, methods and educational systems on the people under their control. As a consequence, education tends to be conducted in English or French rather than in indigenous languages, particularly at the secondary level.

Missionary societies played a key role in developing the educational systems of many of the Commonwealth countries of Africa, and their involvement continues. In most cases their schools have been incorporated into the state system of education. Secondary education was highly selective, geared to producing administrators rather than people with practical skills. Such a tradition dies hard.

There is still considerable British involvement in Commonwealth Africa. The voluntary agencies and missionary societies recruit for Africa, and there are also a significant number of contract teachers in schools and universities subsidised by the Overseas Development Administration.

In many of the former French territories the colonial power assumed complete responsibility for education. There is still considerable French involvement in the educational systems of these countries, with French teachers making up a significant proportion of secondary school staffs. French is the medium of instruction, though there is also a keen interest in learning English.

Two of the largest states on the continent — **Angola** and **Mozambique** — are former Portuguese possessions with Marxist régimes. Their governments are faced with the uphill task of building up their educational system from a low level and fighting a civil war. A peace settlement in Southern Africa should improve matters considerably for both of them. In **Zaire** Belgian influence is still very noticeable.

Virtually every country in Africa has achieved nationhood during the last 20 or 30 years. Yet few of these countries are natural unities. Their boundaries enclose a diversity of tribes, races, languages and religions, and it is a monumental task to reconcile these differences without resorting to force. To be fair, some countries have made remarkable strides forward considering the difficulties they have had to contend with. Others have degenerated into chaos or seem to have lost their way. Many Africans are sensitive to criticism from Westerners, and put much of the blame for their current plight on colonialism.

Africa is very much the Third World. Many countries suffer from poor communications and shortages of equipment and food. If you are posted to the provinces you will need to display resilience and ingenuity. Yet expatriates who manage to make the transition effectively fall in love with Africa and its people, and are reluctant to leave when the time comes.

There is considerable variation. The quality of education seems directly proportional to the wealth of the country, and in this respect **South Africa** comes out top. Here education is virtually universal and educational standards are high — for blacks as well as whites.

For the expatriate there can be considerable variations in the cost of living both within and between countries, and it is wise to get up-to-date information. A course of vaccinations will be necessary against such diseases as cholera and yellow fever, and scrupulous care needs to be given to health matters.

Useful address:

● Association of International Schools in Africa, c/o International School of Kenya, PO Box 14103, Nairobi, Kenya.

Asia

The countries of Asia are remarkably diverse, and most can boast a long and distinguished cultural heritage. While many are regarded as Third World countries, others — such as **Singapore, Taiwan, South Korea** and, above all, **Japan** — are developed and prosperous. Most have well-established educational systems which have been influenced by Western models.

This is one of those areas of the world where teachers are held in very high regard by their pupils, although the high regard is not usually reflected in their salaries. There are few discipline problems in schools and colleges, but on the other hand students tend to be somewhat passive and unwilling to think for themselves. The teacher is regarded as the fount of all wisdom.

Generally speaking, people of this area are polite — certainly to foreigners — and they expect this politeness to be returned. People have to be handled with tact and understanding in order not to cause loss of face. In South East Asia particularly, frankness is equated with rudeness.

SE and E Asians tend to appear reserved and distrustful of shows of affection or temperament. Everyone expects to be treated with respect, no matter what his station in life. This can be very frustrating for the kind of person who likes to let off steam. Many can quote instances of Asians who are so anxious to please that they give the answer you want rather than the correct one!

An appreciation of the religion(s) of the country (Islam, Hinduism or Buddhism), is important, as religion often exerts a strong influence on the lives of the people. Mainstream religious beliefs are often tinged with animism — a belief in the spirit world. There is a tendency to be fatalistic and superstitious, to believe in luck and astrology.

In several countries goods are cheap and plentiful (though this is not the case with **Burma**); labour is cheap, too, and expatriate teachers can often afford a servant or two (but not in **Japan** or **Singapore**). In the urban areas, at least, women seem to be reasonably liberated, and indeed a number of education systems seem to be dominated by women teachers.

The Indian subcontinent is self-sufficient in teachers, so opportunities for expatriates are few and far between. South East Asia is more promising, particularly **Indonesia, Brunei, Malaysia, Singapore** and **Thailand.** The Communist states of **Cambodia, Laos** and **Vietnam** do not appear to make use of Western teachers at present.

Eastern Asia is dominated by the most populous country in the world (**China**) and the most successful (**Japan**).

To understand the Chinese it is important to understand the country's turbulent history. The country, once the most advanced in the world, rested on its laurels for centuries, and when the West arrived with its more advanced ideas and technologies in the last century the country had a rude awakening. This century has been particularly turbulent with the establishment of a republic, civil war and the establishment of a Communist regime by Mao Tse Tung in the late 1940s. Because of the purges of the Cultural Revolution the older Chinese used to be wary of each other and of foreigners, but now there has been a general relaxation of attitudes and contact with foreigners is no longer frowned on.

Family life means a lot to the Chinese. Many families are Confucian in outlook and ancestor worship is part of their tradition. They are generally very hospitable, but one must take care not to offend their sensibilities.

China has developed independently of the West, and by its very size it might seem to be a nation of endless opportunity for the expatriate teacher. In fact, China is a poor country with one of the lowest GNPs per capita in the region. There are some teaching posts, usually in the TEFL field, but the majority are poorly paid volunteer type posts.

Japan, on the other hand, has been exposed to a good deal of Western influence, and since the Second World War this influence has been predominantly American. Yet beneath the surface Japanese society differs markedly from Western society. It is highly competitive with a great deal of pressure put on students to achieve. It is also a strongly conformist and disciplined country, where there is little scope for individualism. It is also very much a man's world. The typical businessman spends his leisure time with his colleagues in bars rather than at home with his wife. Wives of executives tend not to go out to work, but spend much of their time at home worrying about the academic progress of their children.

In Japan there are some well paid jobs, the salaries taking account of the high cost of living, particularly in the large cities.

South Korea and **Taiwan** also have booming economies, and there are certainly opportunities there. But of all the countries of the region **Hong Kong** is probably the one which offers the most openings for British teachers and lecturers. The education system is very much in the British mould. It is also the place where expatriates feel most at

home. Hong Kong has a large foreign community, and first class
amenities. Its main drawbacks are that it is very cramped, and there
is some uncertainty as to what the imminent incorporation into
mainland China will mean for the man and woman in the street.

Australasia and the Pacific
Australia and **New Zealand** will seem like a home from home for many
teachers. However, there is no longer any drive to attract immigrants
on the same scale as in the past, and there are few opportunities in school
teaching for the foreigner, except through an exchange scheme.

The Pacific consists for the most part of small island states a long
way from anywhere. Most have airlinks, but these are expensive, and
you are likely to find yourself existing in a small community with a
very restricted cultural life. But for anyone who enjoys sunshine and
glistening beaches these islands can be paradise.

Some of the larger ones, such as **Fiji,** can offer much more. Fiji ac-
commodates the campus of the University of the South Pacific. **Papua
New Guinea** is a more substantial territory than the others and offers
plenty of interesting terrain. It is also perhaps one of the most fruitful
places to find a job.

The Caribbean
Belize, Suriname, Guiana and **Guyana** fall outside the Spanish/
Portuguese cultural community of Latin America and have much more
in common with the countries of the Caribbean. This area is culturally
very diverse, and the countries reflect their colonial heritage — French,
British, Spanish, Dutch.

The Commonwealth countries are strongly influenced by British ideas
and the British system of education, and universal education is very
much the norm. Often the education system is a partnership between
church schools and the state. The countries have pooled their resources
to finance a regional university, the University of the West Indies, which
has branches on many of the islands.

Some — like **Jamaica, Trinidad and Tobago,** and **Dominica** — are
independent, but many of the smaller ones, like **Bermuda,** are dependencies with a measure of internal self-government. Levels of prosperity
differ widely.

Guiana and the French-speaking islands are dependent territories administered by France. Their tertiary centre is the Université Antilles
Guyane at Cayenne (Guiana). Independent **Haiti** is also French speaking, but this turbulent backward country has few attractions.

There is a small Dutch presence in the area, in **Suriname** (now independent) and the **Netherlands Antilles.** The Dutch-speaking university is situated in Suriname.

The Dominican Republic, once a Spanish colony, has much more in common with South America than its neighbours. Spanish-speaking **Cuba** is somewhat different. The only avowedly Communist country in the Western hemisphere, it is somewhat like Eastern Europe transplanted to the Caribbean. Its brand of education is unique in the area, and has had some major successes — notably in the reduction of illiteracy.

American influence is also strong in the area. The Caribbean is a playground for American tourists, and the island of **Puerto Rico** is in association with the US, although not a state of the union as such.

On the whole, teachers enjoy living in the Caribbean. Most places are readily accessible and the climate good. But it is wrong to look on the islands as a tropical paradise. There is poverty and squalor in the towns and cities and genuine hardship on some of the smaller less prosperous islands.

Europe

Europe is perhaps the most accessible place for any teacher from Great Britain. It is easy to travel to, and in the countries of the European Community there are few, if any, impediments to taking up a job if you are a national of another EC country. In other words, it is quite possible to turn up on spec and look around for a suitable position, except perhaps in the case of **Greece** and **Spain.**

This is not possible in Eastern European countries. Any appointments there are usually handled at the official level by the British Council or the Central Bureau for Educational Visits and Exchanges. And for non-Communist countries outside the EC, such as **Austria, Sweden, Switzerland** and **Turkey,** work permits and visas are usually necessary.

Most European countries are self-sufficient in teachers. While there are opportunities to teach in state secondary schools under exchange schemes administered by the Central Bureau (usually as English assistants), long-term employment is much less common. One reason for this is that foreign teaching qualifications are not recognised in many countries. (After 1992 the position in the EC should change.)

There are exceptions. **Turkey,** for instance, is currently suffering from a shortage of English, maths and science teachers to staff the bi-lingual (Turkish and English medium) schools both in the state and private sectors. This problem should be solved eventually when the country has trained enough teachers of its own.

The private sector, where it exists, is more promising territory for expatriates (particularly TEFL specialists). In some cases a teacher's qualifications have to be approved by the state educational authorities. There are, however, opportunities for teachers of most subjects in

English-medium international schools, of which there is at least one (and often half a dozen or more) in virtually every European capital, including Eastern Europe. The European Community schools (although not strictly speaking private) are a particularly attractive proposition.

The main demand is for TEFL teachers, particularly at the adult level — at British Council Language Institutes, for example. While there are some jobs at public institutions, like the adult evening colleges in **Sweden,** the bulk of the jobs are in the private sector. It is unusual to find a city in Western Europe which does not have at least one private language school specialising in English teaching. Some of these language schools are linked to British institutions like International House; others may be part of a national chain, as is the case in **Italy;** while others may be completely independent. Most insist on a TEFL qualification; a few are prepared to accept virtually anyone, though such institutions are apt to prove unsatisfactory both professionally and salary-wise.

There are also opportunities in higher education, particularly in TEFL and related fields. Many European universities handle their own recruitment, sometimes advertising vacancies, but more often relying on personal contact. The British Council usually handles recruitment for tertiary institutions in Eastern Europe.

In countries where companies are encouraged to provide training for their staff, expatriate teachers may be included on the payroll. The demand is in the main for English tuition, but could also embrace other fields such as management, computers, banking, and so on. This is particularly true of **Germany.**

It remains to be seen whether the thaw in East-West relations will lead to more opportunities for expatriates in the Communist bloc countries of Eastern Europe. **Hungary** seems to be leading the way in this respect with its two English language schools linked up with the private language organisation International House. Similar schemes are planned for both **Poland** and **Czechoslovakia.**

Each European country has a distinctive culture of its own, and adaptability is called for. You cannot count on a large expatriate community if you are living away from the main centres, and knowledge of the local language is highly desirable if you wish to socialise successfully. French is a useful *lingua franca,* and so is German in parts of Eastern and South Eastern Europe.

Latin America

There are more similarities between Latin American countries than differences. One half of the region speaks Spanish; the other half (**Brazil**) speaks Portuguese. All have undergone colonialisation, but most have been independent entities for as long as many European countries.

HTA—G

Christianity is the predominant religion, with Roman Catholicism particularly well entrenched.

While people of European stock may predominate in **Argentina, Costa Rica** and **Uruguay,** in other countries other racial groups form the majority — the South American Indians in the Andean countries. In the north east people are more similar to those in the Caribbean — of mixed African and European stock.

South American society has a strong *machismo* element, which feminists might find trying. Political instability is a problem in certain countries, but actual dictatorships are few and far between. Several are also experiencing economic problems, rampant inflation and massive international debts, but this should cause few headaches to expatriates who are remunerated in hard currency.

While many of the cities, particularly on the Atlantic seaboard, are sophisticated and advanced, there are often extremes of wealth and poverty existing side by side. Some countries are poor and backward, and virtually all have their underdeveloped regions where people live on the breadline. This can be disconcerting to Europeans with a strong social conscience. Yet most people who have lived in Latin America — particularly the cities — find it an exhilarating place. There is ethnic variety, breathtaking scenery, and plenty of *joie de vivre.*

In several of the main cities there are sizeable British communities established for several generations, and in places like these you will often find a private British-style English medium secondary school. In view of the number of US citizens resident in Latin America, American-style international schools are also common.

At the tertiary level there are a number of opportunities for people who can speak the local language, though some of the more technical and scientific subjects may be taught in English. There are posts in the TEFL field, both permanent and short term, usually recruited through the British Council.

In some countries the British Council runs its own English language teaching operations. A more usual pattern is for language institutes to be run by an independent cultural foundation linked to the Council, such as the Sociedade Brasileira de Cultura Inglêsa. The majority of the students tend to be in their teens, and the courses generally lead to Cambridge Lower Certificate and Cambridge Proficiency.

Latin America as a whole lacks teaching personnel at all levels. Various bi-lateral and multi-lateral technical co-operation programmes are endeavouring to make up some of the shortfall. There is also a selective immigration programme administered by the Intergovernmental Committee for Migration (ICM) designed to attract well-qualified Europeans who will provide a stimulus to priority areas of the economy where there is insufficient indigenous talent.

Health warning: Mexico City and a number of cities on the Western side of South America are at high altitudes, and may prove trying for all but the exceptionally fit. There is a risk of malaria in jungle areas, notably in **Brazil, Paraguay** and eastern **Bolivia.**

Reference books:

● *South American Handbook,* Trade & Travel Publications, 5 Prince's Building, George Street, Bath.

● Latin American Newsletters, 61 Old Street, London EC1V 9HX (tel: 01-251 0012) publish *Latin America Weekly Report* as well as five regional reports ten times a year.

Useful address:

● Intergovernmental Committee for Migration (ICM), Geneva Office for Latin America, 17 route des Morillons, PO Box 100, 1211 Geneva 19, Switzerland can help anyone wishing to work in Latin America and publishes a bulletin of job listings which includes teaching posts. Usually these are bachelor status appointments, and knowledge of Spanish or Portuguese is required.

The Middle East and North Africa

This area encompasses the Arab World from **Morocco** in the West to **Oman** in the East plus **Iran** and **Israel.**

The binding force in the Arab world is Islam, though within this framework there are considerable differences between the countries that make up this area with regard to wealth, political orientation and cultural attitude. Very few can claim to be democratic in the Western sense of the word.

Working in the Arab world calls for a large measure of adaptability. One has to be extremely careful to avoid giving offence. Political discussion is to be avoided, particularly in countries like **Libya,** where strong anti-Western attitudes prevail. Above all, be careful to avoid offending people's religious sensibilities.

A study of Islam and its traditions is a prerequisite for anyone visiting the Arab world for the first time. It will enable you to understand the people better, and perhaps appreciate the positive aspects of their religious beliefs which are bound to affect you in some way. This is especially so where attitudes are extremely strict and traditional. In **Saudi Arabia,** for instance, alcohol is forbidden; women are not allowed to drive cars; shops and offices have to close at prayer time; religious police patrol the streets. Not all Europeans, particularly women, can stand the social restrictions. Even in the more liberal countries, the

Ramadan fast is often scrupulously observed, and tempers can get frayed in the heat of the day.

The school system tends to follow the primary-intermediate-secondary pattern. Co-education is rare, and in some countries this can extend to university level. The Koranic system of learning by rote is still quite deeply entrenched in many areas.

The best teaching opportunities in terms of salary occur in the eastern states — **Bahrain, Kuwait, Oman, Qatar, Saudi Arabia** and the **United Arab Emirates** which now boast fine modern cities. Although the salaries and conditions offered are generally more than adequate, many of these posts are on bachelor-status terms. In recent years opportunities have declined slightly, partly due to the fall in the oil price, but also because these countries are now starting to develop expertise among their own nationals.

Expatriate Arabs are much in evidence in the schools of the oil-producing countries, but there is a considerable number of British and other European nationals in the field of TEFL, in bilingual and international schools, working as instructors with oil and aerospace companies, and at the tertiary level. The British Council has several language institutes dotted around this area, and there are a number of private language schools in operation as well.

In North Africa the French influence is still noticeable in **Morocco, Algeria** and **Tunisia.** These countries are virtually self-sufficient in teaching personnel, though there are a number of openings for TEFL specialists. In **Libya,** despite the government's hostility to Britain, there is still a sizeable contingent of teachers from Britain, and this is also true of **Egypt.**

There are opportunities in the other countries of the Arab world, notably in international schools and at the tertiary level. The sad exception is **Lebanon,** once the cultural centre of the region, which has degenerated into chaos. Prospects in **Iraq** have improved since the cessation of the conflict with Iran.

Iran stands apart culturally from the Arab world. In the days of the Shah there was a significant expatriate presence in education, but this has disappeared. Nowadays expatriates are definitely not welcome, but this could change.

Useful addresses:
- United Nations Relief and Works Agency for Palestinian Refugees (UNRWA), Postfach 700, Vienna, Austria.
- Near East/South Asia Council of Overseas Schools, c/o American College of Greece, PO Box 60018, 153 10 Aghia Paraskevi, Attikis, Greece.

North America

See individual entries on **Canada** and the **USA** in the next section.

COUNTRY INFORMATION A-Z

This section sets out to provide you with brief information about most of the countries which employ foreign teachers. The population is usually given as well as the GNP per capita, which is a rough measure of the prosperity of the country in question.

At least one address is given from which you can seek further information on teaching opportunities in that particular country. In the case of embassies and high commissions the person you should normally contact is the cultural attaché or educational attaché.

Mention is made of some, but by no means all, of the agencies that recruit regularly for a particular country. However, in some cases the number of posts they handle is very small and there is no guarantee that they will be handling any in a particular year.

Note also that information of this nature quickly goes out of date. Recruitment policies change, revolutions occur, embassies move to new premises, and so on. The information is correct at the time of writing (early 1989), but is no guide to the future.

AFGHANISTAN   Pop: 17.5m   Area: 647,000 sq km
GNP: $160
Embassy: 31 Prince's Gate, London SW7 1QQ (tel: 01-589 8891).
Ministry of Education: Char Raki Malek Ashgar, Kabul.

The political future in Afghanistan is somewhat unclear following the Russian pull-out. If matters return to normal there may well be opportunities for foreign teachers and lecturers from the West. The educational system is relatively undeveloped except in the main towns with adult literacy around 20%. There are universities at Kabul and Nangarhar and state secondary schools in provincial capitals.

ALGERIA   Pop: 23m   Area: 2.4m sq km   GNP: $2,380
Embassy: 54 Holland Park, London W11 3RS (tel: 01-221 7800).
Consulate: 6 Hyde Park Gate, London SW7 5EW (tel: 01-221 7800).
Ministry of Education: 8 ave de Pékin, Mouradia, Algiers.

Education follows the traditional French pattern modified to suit local circumstances. All the schools are state run. There is an American School in Algiers and the British Council has a language institute here. There are sometimes opportunities in TEFL in the universities situated in Algiers, Boumerdes, Constantine, Annaba, Oran, Sétif.
Recruitment: British Council; ECIS.

ANGOLA   Pop: 9m   Area: 1.25m sq km   GNP: $500
Embassy: 87 Jermyn Street, London SW1 (tel: 01-839 5743).
Ministry of Education: Avda Comte Jika, Luanda.

This former Portuguese possession has been plagued by civil war but a solution may now have been found. Teaching opportunities exist, notably at the British Council's language institute in Luanda. Other opportunities may exist at the Universidade Agostinho Neto in Luanda and with foreign oil companies operating in the country.
Recruitment: British Council.

ANGUILLA   Pop: 7,000   Area: 90 sq km
Education Department: The Secretariat, The Valley.

This British dependency in the Caribbean boasts six primary schools and one secondary school.
Recruitment: VSO.

ANTIGUA & BARBUDA   Pop: 81,500   Area: 440 sq km
GNP: $1,830
High Commission: 15 Thayer Street, London W1M 5DL(tel: 01-486 7073).
Ministry of Education, Culture and Youth Affairs: Church Street, St John's.

Opportunities sometimes arise in secondary schools, of which there are sixteen. The State Island College provides technical and teacher training, and there is an extramural department of the University of the West Indies here.
Recruitment: VSO.

ARGENTINE REPUBLIC   Pop: 31m   Area: 2.77m sq km
GNP: $2,470
Embassy: Brazilian Embassy (Argentine Interests Section), 111 Cadogan Gardens, London SW3 (tel: 01-730 4388).
Ministry of Education: Pizzurno 935, 1020 Buenos Aires.

Argentina has one of the highest standards of education in South America. It also has a sizeable British colony which has lived in the country for several generations. As a result the country has three well established British-type English medium schools, St George's, St Andrew's and St Hilda's, all in Buenos Aires. Other international schools include Barker College, Belgrano Day School, and the American Community School (Association Escuelas Lincoln). In Cordoba there is the Reydon School for Girls. There are Anglo-Argentinian Cultural Institutes in all the major cities offering English language tuition. The

country has over 29 state and 23 private universities — notably in Buenos Aires, Cordoba, Catamarca, Cuyo, Entre Rios, Jujuy, La Pampa, Patagonia, La Plata, Litora, Tandil.
Recruitment: ECIS; International House.

AUSTRALIA   Pop: 16m   Area: 7.7m sq km   GNP:$11,890
High Commission: Australia House, Strand, London WC2B 4LA (tel: 01-438 8193).

The country boasts some 7,500 government schools; 2,454 non-government schools; 19 universities; 47 colleges and institutes of advanced education (vocationally-oriented education); 271 technical and FE colleges. However, Australia is virtually self-sufficient in teachers. Primary and secondary education is in the hands of the different states. For information on posts in secondary schools it is advisable to contact the various ministries of education direct.
    Federal State Departments of Education:
New South Wales: GPO Box 33, Sydney, NSW 2001
Western Australia: 151 Royal Street, East Perth, WA 6000
Victoria: 2 Treasury Place, Melbourne, VIC 3002
Queensland: Old Treasury Building, Queen Street, Brisbane, QLD 400
South Australia: 9th Floor, 31 Flinders Street, Adelaide, SA 5000
Northern Territories: T & G Building, 69 Smith Street, Darwin NT 5794
Tasmania: 116 Bathurst Street, Hobart, TAS 7001
Australian Capital Territory: PO Box 826, Woden, ACT 2606
    Opportunities occur in the tertiary sector, and advertisements for these positions appear frequently in the *Times Higher Education Supplement. Currently there is also a demand for TEFL teachers to teach immigrants.*
Recruitment: ACU; League for the Exchange of Commonwealth Teachers.

AUSTRIA   Pop: 7.5m   Area: 84,000 sq km   GNP: $9,140
Austrian Embassy: 18 Belgrave Mews West, London SW1X 5HU (tel: 01-235 3731).
The Austrian Institute: 28 Rutland Gate, London SW7 1PQ
Ministry of Education: Minoritenplatz 5, A-1014 Vienna

Teachers in the state system are civil servants and have to be Austrian nationals, but a teacher exchange is in operation. There are opportunities in private schools, adult institutes, various private language institutes and Austria's twelve universities for English teachers. Vienna has two international schools, the American International School (Salmanndörferstrasse 47) and the Vienna International School (Strasse der Menschenrechte 1). Innsbruck has an international high school and Salzburg an international preparatory school.

Austria is not a member of the EC, and work permits must be obtained by the employer in Austria prior to the employee's departure from the UK (except in case of exchange teachers), and the work permit application has to be sent to the consular section of the Austrian Embassy. You should register with the police within 24 hours of arrival, and if staying more than six months a residence permit must be obtained.

Recruitment: Central Bureau; ECIS; Inlingua.

BAHAMAS   Pop: 235,000   Area: 14,000 sq km
GNP: $4,260
High Commission: 10 Chesterfield Street, London W1X 8AH (tel: 01-408 4488).
Ministry of Education: Shirley Street, PO Box N3913, Nassau.

There are state and private secondary schools — all English medium — including Freeport High School and St Paul's Methodist College in Freeport; Kingsway Academy, St Andrew's School, St Anne's Parish School and St John's College in Nassau. There is also the College of the Bahamas, a junior community college affiliated to the University of the West Indies and some American universities, which offers associate degree programmes to some 3,000 students.

Recruitment: League for the Exchange of Commonwealth Teachers; ECIS.

BAHRAIN   Pop: 435,000   Area: 622 sq km   GNP: $10,480
Embassy: 98 Gloucester Road, London SW7 4AU (tel: 01-370 5978)
Ministry of Education: PO Box 43, Khalid bin Al-Walid Road, Qudhaibiya, Manama.

Bahrain is perhaps the most cosmopolitan of the Gulf states, and has a well-established educational system. There are opportunities in most subjects in private international schools, such as Bahrain School (PO Box 934), Habara School (PO Box 26516) and St Christopher's School (PO Box 32052). A number of expatriates are employed by the tertiary institutions: the Arabian Gulf University, the University College of Arts, Science and Education, the Gulf Polytechnic and the College of Health Sciences. There are a number of private language schools, such as Polyglot, the Gulf Academy and Gulf Language Services. The Government and companies such as Gulf Air and the Bahrain Petroleum Co provide in-service training for their employees.

Recruitment: British Council; ECIS.

BANGLADESH   Pop: 108m   Area: 144,000 sq km
GNP: $162
High Commission: 28 Queen's Gate, London SW7 5JA (tel: 01-584
   0081).
Ministry of Education: Bangladesh Secretariat, Bhaban 7, 2nd 9-Storey
   Building, 6th Floor, Dhaka.

There is very little expatriate involvement in the state sector or in English
language teaching. There may be opportunities in English medium
schools such as the American International School and St Francis
Xavier's Greenherald International School. There are universities at
Dhaka, Rajshahi, Chittagong, Jahnagirnagar, an Engineering University at Dhaka and an Agricultural University at Mymensingh staffed
almost exclusively by Bangladeshis.
Recruitment: British Council; VSO.

BARBADOS   Pop: 250,000   Area: 430 sq km   GNP: $4,560
High Commission: 1 Great Russell Street, London WC1B 3NH (tel:
   01-631 4975).
Ministry of Education and Culture: Jemmot's Lane, St Michael.

One of the most prosperous islands of the Caribbean, Barbados has
a well developed schools system. There are 21 government secondary
schools and 15 private ones, a polytechnic, a teacher training college,
a technical institute and the Cave Hill Campus of the University of the
West Indies.

BELGIUM   Pop: 10m   Area: 30,500 sq km   GNP: $8,430
Embassy: 103 Eaton Square, London SW1 9AB (tel: 01-235 5422)
Ministry of Education (Flemish Sector): Centre Arts Lux, 4th and 5th
   Floors, 58 ave des Arts, BP 5, 1040 Brussels.
Ministry of Education (French Sector): 68a rue du Commerce, 1040
   Brussels.

The Embassy publishes useful notes on living conditions and administrative procedures.
   Apart from having Flemish medium schools and French medium
ones, there are two separate educational systems; the écoles officielles
(state-owned) and the écoles libres (privately owned but subsidised by
the state). Although there are no opportunities in state schools, except
under teacher exchange schemes, there are schools for service children,
and for the children of European Community employees, as well as
private international schools catering for expatriate children. They
include:
British School of Brussels, 19 Steenweg op Leuven, 1980 Tervuren

Le Verseau International School (French/English medium) 60 Rue de Wavre, 1301 Bierges

British Primary School, 6 Stationstraat, Vossem (Tervuren)

International School of Brussels, 19 Kattenberg, Brussels 1170

International School of Liege, 64 Rue Pierre Henvard, 4920 Embourg

Antwerp International School, 180 Veltwijeklan, 2070 Erkeren

St John's International School, 146 Dreve Richelle, 1410 Waterloo

EEC International School, 103 Boulevard Louis Schmidt, 1040 Brussels

Brussels English Primary School, 23 Avenue Franklin Roosevelt, 1050 Brussels

SHAPE International School, Mons.

There are opportunities in language schools and universities, particularly Vesalius College, a new English language medium college linked to the Flemish Free University of Brussels. (Address: 2 Pleinlaan, 1050 Brussels.)

The Bulletin, 329 Avenue Moliere, 1060 Brussels carries vacancy advertisements.

No work permit or visa is required for EC nationals. Within eight days of arrival you should report your intended place of resdence to the local town hall to obtain a certificate of registration (CIRE) valid for one year, or a three-month provisional certificate.

Recruitment: Central Bureau; ECIS; Inlingua; SCEA.

BELIZE   Pop: 170,000   Area: 23,000 sq km   GNP: $1,200
High Commission: 15 Thayer Street, London W1M 5DL (tel: 01-486 8381).
Ministry of Education: Belmopan, Belize.

Situated on the east coast of Central America, Belize with a population of less than 200,000 has 225 primary schools and 23 secondary schools. Post secondary institutions include the University College of Belize, a teachers' college, a school of nursing and a technical college. A work permit is necessary and is applied for by the employer on behalf of the employee.

Recruitment: VSO.

BENIN   Pop: 4m   Area: 113,000 sq km   GNP: $300
Consulate: 125/129 High Street, Edgware, Middx HA8 7HS (tel: 01-951 1234).
Ministry of Primary Education: Porto Novo.
Ministry of Secondary and Higher Education: Cotonou.

Formerly Dahomey. The educational system follows the French system and the adult literacy rate stands at 25%. The International Develop-

ment Association and OPEC Development Fund are assisting in educational improvements, including teacher training. There are opportunities in TEFL at the University of Benin, Porto Novo.
Recruitment: British Council.

BERMUDA   Pop: 78,000   Area: 53 sq km   GNP: $16,300
Ministry of Education: Old Hospital Building, 7 Point Finger Road, Paget.

This prosperous group of 150 islands is still a colony with its own representative government. There are nine private and government secondary schools, including Bermuda High School (in Pembroke), Mount St Agnes Academy and Saltus Grammar School (both in Hamilton). Bermuda College offers post secondary education.
Recruitment: ECIS.

BHUTAN   Pop: 1.3m   Area: 45,000 sq km   GNP: $140
Ministry of Education: Thimpu.

Only 20% of children attend school in this remote Himalayan kingdom. There are eight high schools, one junior college, six technical schools and one higher education institute. There are no private schools. English is the medium of instruction and a British-type syllabus is followed. The country has a large number of expatriate teachers, mostly Indian.
Recruitment: VSO.

BOLIVIA   Pop: 6.25m   Area: 1.1m sq km   GNP: $400
Embassy: 160 Eaton Square, London SW1 9AD (tel: 01-235 2257).
Ministry of Education: Avda Arce, La Paz.

Opportunities exist in private schools, particularly for science and maths teachers. These include Cochamba Co-operative School, La Paz American Co-operative School, Orura Anglo-American School and Santa Cruz Co-operative School. The Ministry of Education in La Paz can provide further information. La Paz University is the most important tertiary sector institution. The oldest is St Francis Xavier University founded in 1624.

BOTSWANA   Pop: 1m   Area: 582,000 sq km   GNP: $920
High Commission: 8 Stratford Place, London W1N 9AE (tel: 01-499 0031).
Ministry of Education: Private Bag 005, Gaborone.

This large country with a small population is making great strides forward with its education system. The current pattern of 7 years primary-2

years intermediate-3 years senior secondary is now changing to a 6-3-3-system. There is virtually universal education at the primary level and the government aims to provide universal education at intermediate level by the 1990s. Northside School in Gaborone is the main international establishment. At the tertiary level there is the University of Botswana and Molepole College of Education. Most educational institutions have expatriate teachers on their staffs.
Recruitment: British Council; IVS; ODA.

BRAZIL   Pop: 138m   Area: 8.5m sq km   GNP: $1,610
Embassy: 32 Green Street, London W1Y 4AT (tel: 01-499 0877)
Consulate: 6 Deanery Street, London W1Y 5LH.
Ministry of Education: Esplanada dos Ministeriós, Bloco L, 70.444
   Brasilia DF.

Portuguese-speaking Brazil is the giant of the South American continent. It has some of the largest cities including Rio de Janeiro and São Paolo with highly developed educational systems. In rural areas educational provsion is not as good. The north east region, for example, still has only 55% adult illiteracy.

There are a number of international schools in Belem, Belo Horizonte, Campina, Curitiba, Porto Alegre, Recife and Salvador. There are two in Rio de Janeiro (the American School and the British School) and four in São Paulo (including St Paul's School, 166 Jardim Paulistino). Many large Anglo-Brazilian cultural centres (Sociedade Brasileira de Cultura Inglesa) flourish in the major cities. The society in Rio, for instance, has eighteen branches in the city plus two in Brasilia. There are also a number of Brasil-American foundations involved in English language teaching. There are no less than 67 universities in the country, of which 20 are privately owned. For information on teaching at university level contact CAPES, Recrutamento de Recursos Humanos no Exterior SAS, Quadra 6, Lote 4, Bloco L, 4° andar, 70.000 Brasilia DF.

For information on work permits and diploma recognition contact the Secretaria de Assuntos Internacionais, Ministério de Educãçao, Esplanada do Ministérios, Bloco L, 8° andar, 70.074 Brasilia DF.
Recruitment: British Council; ECIS; International House.

BRUNEI   Pop: 222,000   Area: 5,765 sq km   GNP: $15,989
High Commission: 49 Cromwell Road, London SW7 2ED (tel: 01-581
   0521).
Ministry of Education: Lapangan Terbang Lama Berakas.

This small, oil-rich sultanate has both state and private schools which may be Malay medium, English medium, Arabic medium or Chinese medium. There are also vocational and technical schools, as well as a brand new university. The Centre for British Teachers (CBT) has a large programme here both at the secondary level and the pre-university level. The Brunei Shell Petroleum Co operate a primary school for expatriates at Seria and there is an international school at Bandar Seri Begawan.

BULGARIA   Pop: 9m   Area: 111,000 sq km   GNP: $4,150
Embassy: 186 Queen's Gate, London SW7 5HL (tel: 01-584 9400).
Ministry of National Education: Blvd A Stamboliisky 18, 1000 Sofia.

There are a few foreign TEFL teachers here who have been recruited through official channels both in schools and in the country's three universities at Sofia, Veliko Turnovo and Plovdiv. There is an international school, the Anglo American School of Sofia.
Recruitment: British Council; Central Bureau; ECIS.

BURKINA FASO   Pop: 8m   Area: 274,000 sq km
GNP: $160
Honorary Consulate: 150 Buckingham Palace Road, London SW1W 9SA (tel: 01-730 8141)
Ministry of National Education: BP 7032, Ouagadougou.
Ministry of Higher Education: BP 7130, Ouagadougou.

Formerly Upper Volta. With World Bank help the country has radically reformed its education system in rural areas with the establishment of 750 centres combining elementary schooling with agricultural training. This should help to reduce the adult illiteracy rate of 86%. There is an International School at Ouagadougou (BP 35) as well as the University of Ouagadougou where there may be TEFL opportunities. The Ministry of Education has a British Council recruited adviser.
Recruitment: British Council.

BURMA   Pop: 37.5m   Area: 676,000 sq km   GNP: $180
Embassy: 19a Charles Street, Berkeley Square, London W1X 8ER (tel: 01-499 8841).
Ministry of Education: Ministers' Office, Rangoon.

Burma is a country where time seems to have stood still, and this applies very much to the educational system. English is not widely used as a medium of instruction and there is little expatriate involvement in either education or business life, except at the International School of Rangoon. There are two universities, at Rangoon and Mandalay.
Recruitment: British Council.

BURUNDI   Pop: 5m   Area: 29,000 sq km   GNP: $250
Honorary Consulate: 19 Kenton Park Crescent, Harrow, Middx.
Ministry of Education: Bujumbura.

Opportunities could exist at the university of Burundi at Bujumbura.
Recruitment: British Council.

CAMBODIA (KAMPUCHEA)   Pop: 7m   Area: 181,000 sq km
GNP: $70
Ministry of Education: Phnom Penh.

Until some agreement can be reached over the country's future no
teaching opportunities are likely because of the uneasy political situation, although Oxfam is active on development projects there. In the
past expatriates with mission backing have worked in Cambodian
refugee camps in Thailand and in zones near the Thai border controlled
by the Khmer People's National Liberation Front (KPNLF — British
Office: 63 Winn Road, London SE12, tel: 01-857 0395), but this can
be hazardous.

CAMEROON   Pop: 10m   Area: 475,000 sq km   GNP: $800
Embassy: 84 Holland Park, London W11 3SB (tel: 01-727 0771).
Ministry of National Education: Yaounde.
Ministry of Higher Education: Yaounde.

There are two distinct patterns of education which date from the colonial era: the western part follows the British system, the rest of the
country follows the French system. There are plans to harmonise the
two which are taking a long time to implement. Two thirds of the
children receive primary education — quite a high proportion for Africa
— and some 38% of the schools are under mission or private owner-
ship. There is an International School at Douala (BP 1909) and an
American School at Yaounde (BP 7475). At the tertiary level there is
the University of Yaounde and the École Nationale Superieure
Polytechnique.
Recruitment: British Council; Christians Abroad; ECIS.

CANADA: Pop: 26m   Area: 10m sq km   GNP: $13,140
High Commission: Canada House, Trafalgar Square, London SW1Y
    5BJ and 1 Grosvenor Square, London W1X 0AB (tel: 01-629 9492).

Canada is oversupplied with teachers, and consequently teaching positions for foreigners are hard to come by, except in the case of exchange
teachers. It is usually only possible for a work permit to be issued if
the local Canada Employment Centre is convinced that there is no

suitably qualified Canadian national available to fill a post for which a foreign teacher has been accepted. The most fruitful areas for vacancies are in the North West Territories and the remoter parts of Saskatchewan and Alberta.

There are international schools in Ottawa, Toronto, Vancouver and Windsor, Nova Scotia. The Leicester Pearson United World College of the Pacific is at Victoria, BC.

Sources of Information
● The High Commission keeps a list of current vacancies in its reception area, but these do not usually include teaching posts. Government offices for the various provinces provide similar information, but do not necessarily recruit. *Alberta:* 1 Mount Street, London W1; *British Columbia:* 1 Regent Street, London SW1Y 4NS; *Newfoundland:* 60 Trafalgar Square, London SW1; *Nova Scotia:* 14 Pall Mall, London SW1Y 5LU; *Ontario:* 21 Knightsbridge, London SW1X 1LY; *Quebec:* 59 Pall Mall, London SW1 5JH; *Saskatchewan:* 21 Pall Mall, London SW1.
● Canadian Education Association, Suite 8-200, 252 Bloor Street West, Toronto, Ontario M5S 1V5 (issues a leaflet *Information for teachers thinking of coming to Canada*).
● Canadian Teachers' Federation, 110 Argyle Street, Ottowa, Ontario K2P 1B4 (issues a booklet *Teaching in Canada*).
● Canadian Association of Independent Schools, c/o Appleby College, Oakville, Ontario L6K 3P1.
● Canadian Association of University Teachers, Suite 1001, 75 Albert Street, Ottawa, Ontario K1P 5E7 (advertises vacancies in the *CAUT Bulletin*).
● Association of Universities and Colleges of Canada, 151 Slater Street, Ottawa, Canada K1P 5N1 (publishes vacancies in *University Affairs*).
Recruitment: ACU; Central Bureau (for Quebec); League for the Exchange of Commonwealth Teachers.

CAYMAN ISLANDS   Pop: 20,000   Area: 256 sq km
GNP: $8,333
Government Office: 17b Curzon Street, London W1 (tel: 01-408 2482).
Department of Education: George Town, Grand Cayman.

Around 200 expatriate teachers are currently employed by the Cayman Islands Government, private schools and the International College of the Cayman Islands, Newlands, Grand Cayman. There is also a community college. The three islands are a British dependency, and no visas are required for British and Commonwealth passport holders. Teachers

working in the private sector will need to obtain work permits and register with the Department of Education.
Recruitment: Crown Agents.

CENTRAL AFRICAN REPUBLIC   Pop: 2.7m   Area: 623,000 sq km   GNP: $280
Ministry of National Education: BP 791, Bangui.

The educational system is based on the French model. No recruitment is conducted in the UK, but there may be opportunities for English-speaking expatriates at the University of Bangui, BP 1450, Bangui.

CHAD   Pop: 5m   Area: 1.3m sq km   GNP: $88
Ministry of National Education: N'Djamena.

This is a desperately poor country which exists largely on aid. French influence is strong, but there is an American International School at N'Djamena. There may be opportunities for non-Francophone teachers at the University of Chad, BP 1117, N'Djamena.

CHILE   Pop: 12m   Area: 757,000 sq km   GNP: $1,590
Embassy: 33 Regent Street, London SW1 (tel: 01-734 0802/3).
Ministry of Education: Avda Liberator B o'Higgins 1371, Santiago.

There are several international schools here: the Colegio Ingles St John's, Concepción; the American School, Puerto Montt; MacKay School and St Margaret's School for Girls in Viña del Mar; Grange School, International School, Lincoln International Academy and Redland School in Santiago. The Anglo Chileno Cultural Association flourishes in many towns, and there is a British-type school in Santiago known as the Grange School. There are a number of flourishing universities, notably in Santiago (University of Chile, Catholic University of Chile), Atacama, Antofagasta, Bibío, Concepción, La Serena, Talca, Valdivia and Valparaiso.
Recruitment: Central Bureau; British Council; ECIS; S American Missionary Society.

CHINA   Pop: 1,035m   Area: 9.5m sq km   GNP: $330
Embassy: 49-51 Portland Place, London W1N 3AH (tel: 01-636 5726).
Consular Section: 31 Portland Place, London W1N 3AG.
Cultural Section: 28 College Crescent, London NW3.
Education Commission: 37 Damuchang Hutong, Xicheng District, Beijing.

The most populous country of the world, China is nevertheless a Third

World country with few natural resources. The country is now keen
to have expatriate teachers, notably in the TEFL field, but cannot afford them. Most opportunities are therefore on a volunteer basis. A
number of agencies recruit for China. One of these is the Amity Foundation scheme operated by the British Council of Churches which places
TEFL teachers in tertiary institutions. These are not missionary posts
as such, and the incumbents are not expected to proselytise. There is
an International School in Beijing and American Schools in Guangzhou
and Shanghai.
Recruitment: Bell; British Council; VSO; British Council of Churches.

COLOMBIA   Pop: 28m   Area: 1.1m sq km   GNP: $1,430
Embassy: 3 Hans Crescent, London SW1X 0LR (tel: 01-589 9177).
Consulate: 140 Park Lane, London W1Y 3DF (tel: 01-493 4565).
Ministry of Education: Centro Administrativo Nacional, 501 Avda El
    Dorado, Bogotá.

There are international schools in Baranquilla (British American School,
Colegio Karl C Parrish), Bogotá (Anglo Colombian School, English
School), Cali (Colegio Colombo Britanico), Cartagena (George
Washington School), Medellin (Columbus School). The British Coun-
cil has a language institute at Bogotá. Colombia has over 200 tertiary
level institutions, many of them with US backing.
Recruitment: British Council; Central Bureau; ECIS; International
House.

COMORES ISLANDS   Pop: 415,000   Area: 2,171 sq km
GNP: $340
Ministry of National Education: BP 446, Moroni.

This former French territory situated in the Indian Ocean between
Madagascar and the African mainland is self sufficient in primary
school teachers but employs French-speaking teachers at the secondary
level. The island of Mayotte which forms part of the archipelago has
opted to remain part of France.
Recruitment: Africa Inland Mission.

CONGO   Pop: 1.7m   Area: 342,000 sq km   GNP: $1,120
Honorary Consulate: Livingstone House, 11 Carteret Street, London
    SW1H 9DH (tel: 01-222 7575).
Ministry of Education: BP 169, Brazzaville.

There is no private education sector in this former French possession,
which boasts one of the highest literacy rates in Africa: 63%. The

Marien Ngouabi University in the capital is the main tertiary level institution.
Recruitment: British Council.

COSTA RICA   Pop: 2.7m   Area: 51,000 sq km   GNP: $1,280
Embassy: 93 Star Street, London W2 1QF (tel: 01-723 1772).
Ministry of Education: Apdo 10,087, San José.

Costa Rica is one of the most stable and developed countries in Central America and perhaps the most European in character. There are several international schools in San José including the Anglo-American School (PO Box 3188), Costa Rica Academy (PO Box 4941), Lincoln School (PO Box 1919). At the tertiary level there is: University of Central America, University of Costa Rica (both in San José), the University of Herdeia and the Open University.

Documentation required for residence and work permits: Letter of application, contract, references, birth certificate, marriage certificate, police record or good conduct declaration signed by three witnesses, chest X-ray and blood test reports, photocopies of used pages in passport, six front and six profile photographs and an international money order for US$20.
Recruitment: Central Bureau; ECIS.

CUBA   Pop: 10m   Area: 111,000 sq km   GNP: $2,696
Embassy: 167 High Holborn, London WC1 (tel: 01-240 2488).
Ministry of Education: Obispo No 160, Havana.

Since the revolution Cuba has virtually eradicated illiteracy and increased educational provision. Over 85% of Cubans now receive a secondary education, higher than in most Latin American countries. Education is based on Marxist-Leninist principles and combines study with manual work, particularly at tertiary level. More than 250,000 students are said to be receiving higher education. The small Foreign Students' School in Havana (c/o British Embassy) serves the expatriate community. There are universities at Havana, Santiago de Cuba, Santa Clara and Camagüey.

CYPRUS   Pop: 665,000   Area: 9,250 sq km   GNP: $4,035.
High Commission: 93 Park Street, London W1Y 4ET (tel: 01-499 8272).
Ministry of Education: Nicosia.
Turkish Rep of N Cyprus Office: 28 Cockspur Street, London SW1 (tel: 01-837 4577).
Ministry of Education: Lefkosa.

Cyprus is a divided country politically. There is the Turkish Republic of Cyprus in the north of the island, and the Republic of Cyprus in the south. A rapprochement between Greece and Turkey may help to ease the situation in coming years.

International and English medium schools can be found at Larnaca (American Academy, PO Box 112); Limassol (Limassol Grammar School (Homer Street), Logos School of English Education (PO Box 1075)); Nicosia (American Academy, Falcon School, Grammar School); Paphos (Anglo-American International School). There are several private language schools teaching English plus the British Council's own institute. Most other educational institutions are state-run except for the English School which used to have links with the British Council and is now run by a foundation. There is also a school attached to the British base. At the tertiary level there is the University College of Arts and Science in Limassol and the Pedagogical Academy. There are also government-run adult evening institutes. A university opened in the Turkish part of the island in 1986.
Recruitment: British Council; SCEA.

CZECHOSLOVAKIA   Pop: 15.5m   Area: 128,000 sq km
GNP: $8,280
Embassy: 25 Kensington Palace Gardens, London W8 4QY (tel: 01-727 3966/7).
Ministry of Education: Prague.

The demand is for people with TEFL expertise, but recruitment is conducted only at an official level usually for the five universities: Prague (Charles University), Bratislava (Comenius), Olomouc (Palacky), Kosice (Safárik), Brno (Purkyne). There are 27 government run language institutes in the principal towns and the British Council runs summer schools of English mainly for teachers. Prague has an International School (c/o US Embassy).
Recruitment: British Council; ECIS.

DENMARK   Pop: 5m   Area: 43,000 sq km   GNP: $11,290
Embassy: 55 Sloane Street, London SW1X 9SR (tel: 01-235 1255)
Ministry of Education: Frederiksholms Kanal 25D, DK-1220 Copenhagen K.

The International Relations Division of the Ministry publishes a booklet on the Danish educational system and regulations governing the employment of foreign teachers. Generally speaking a foreign teacher can only be employed in state schools in a temporary capacity until he or she takes a supplementary qualifying examination.

The provision of primary and lower secondary education in the Folkeskoler is the responsibility of the local authorities (Kommunal-bestyrelse). The upper secondary schools (Gymnasia) are administered by the counties (Amtsrad), and applications should be made to the appropriate authority. There are also a number of private institutions which are not subject to the same regulations. Information about employment in the private sector is obtainable from Frie Grundskolers Faellesrad, Nygade 6, DK-4200 Slagelse. There are a few international schools: Aarhus (Interskolen); Copenhagen (International School, Rygaards International School); Esbjerg (International School); Svendborg (International School). Denmark has five universities, at Copenhagen, Aarhus, Aalborg, Odense and Roskilde. It also has a well developed system of adult education centres independent of the state known as Folk High Schools. Details are available from Efterskolernes Sekretariat, Farvergarde 27, DK-1463 Copenhagen-K. Finally there are several private language schools.

EC citizens are allowed to work in Denmark for three months. At least two weeks before the end of this period you should apply to the Department of Aliens for a residence and work permit.

Useful Address: Direktoratet for Udlaendinge, Absolonsgade 9, 1658 Copenhagen V.

Further Reading: The ICU, Bremerholm 6, 4th Floor, 1069 Copenhagen K publish a useful booklet entitled *Guide for Young Visitors to Denmark.* It would also be useful for the not-so-young.

Recruitment: ECIS; Inlingua; Central Bureau.

DJIBOUTI   Pop: 405,000   Area: 22,000 sq km   GNP: $480
Ministry of Education: BP 2101, Djibouti.

Two ethnic groups live in this territory: the Issa (of Somali origin) and the Afar (of Ethiopian origin). There are nineteen secondary schools, many of them private, and a teacher training college. Official languages are Arabic and French, and French influence is strong.

DOMINICA   Pop: 75,000   Area: 751 sq km   GNP: $1,150
High Commission: 1 Collingham Gardens, London SW5 0HW (tel: 01-370 5194).
Ministry of Education: Government Headquarters, Kennedy Avenue, Roseau.

There are both government and church schools on the island, together with a teacher training college, a technical college and a branch of the University of the West Indies.

Recruitment: VSO.

DOMINICAN REPUBLIC   Pop: 6.5m   Area: 48,000 sq km   GNP: $1,090
Honorary Consulate: 6 Queen's Mansions, Brook Green, London W6 7EB (tel: 01-602 1885).
Ministry of Education: Avda Máximo Gómez, Santo Domingo, DN.

Sharing an island with Haiti this country was first a Spanish colony and then a French colony. There are international schools at Jarabacoa (Escuela Caribe); La Romana (Abraham Lincoln School); Santo Domingo (Carol Morgan Schools). The Republic has six universities including the University of Santo Domingo founded in 1538.

ECUADOR   Pop: 9.4m   Area: 284,000 sq km   GNP: $1,220
Embassy: 3 Hans Crescent, London SW1X 0LS (tel: 01-534 2648).
Ministry of Education: Méjia 348, Quito.

Ecuador has a mix of state and private schools, and it is in the private sector that opportunities exist, mainly for English teachers. There are language schools (including one run by the British Council in Quito) and seventeen tertiary level institutions. International schools exist at Guyaquil (American School, Inter-American Academy); Quito (American International School, Alliance Academy).
Recruitment: British Council; CIIR; CIME.

EGYPT   Pop: 50m   Area: 1m sq km   GNP: $610
Embassy: 26 South Street, London W1 8EL (tel: 01-493 6306).
Consulate: 19 Kensington Palace Gardens, London W8 (tel: 01-229 8818).
Egyptian Education Bureau: 4 Chesterfield Gardens, London W1Y 8BR.
Ministry of Education: 6 Amin Samy Street, El-Sayed El-Zeinab, Cairo.

Egypt is a major exporter of teachers to other countries in the Arab world. There are, however, opportunities for TEFL teachers in private schools, language schools (including British Council operations), and teacher training colleges. International education is provided by the Schutz American School in Alexandria (PO Box 1000), and by the British International School (PO Box 137), Cairo American College (PO Box 39) and the Heliopolis International School — all in Cairo. There are universities at Alexandria, Assiut, Cairo, Mansoura, Menia, Ismailia, Tanta and Zagazig. The American University of Cairo enjoys a particularly high reputation.
Recruitment: British Council; ECIS; International House; VSO.

EL SALVADOR   Pop: 5.5m   Area: 21,000 sq km
GNP: $880
Embassy: 62 Welbeck Street, London W1 (tel: 01-486 8182/3).
Ministry of Education: Calle Delgado y 8a Avde Norte, San Salvador.

The best opportunities here exist in the private sector at such schools
as the Academia Britanica Cuscatleca (PO Box 121, Santa Tecla) and
the Escuela Americana (PO Box 01-35, San Salvador). There are four
universities including the University of El Salvador. Normally your
employer should obtain a work permit for you in El Salvador before
you can obtain a temporary residence visa through a Salvadorean consulate. In certain cases it is possible to enter the country with a tourist
visa and obtain temporary residence once you arrive. This is, however,
at the discretion of the Ministry of the Interior.
Recruitment: British Council; ECIS; ICM.

ETHIOPIA   Pop: 42m   Area: 1.2m sq km   GNP: $110
Embassy: 17 Princes Gate, London SW7 1PZ (tel: 01-589 7212).
Ministry of Education: PO Box 1176, Addis Ababa.

Drought and civil war are just two of the problems that the Marxist-
orientated government has to cope with, and educational plans have
therefore been set back. There are a number of expatriates, including
Indians and British, teaching in schools, often on volunteer terms. There
may be opportunites at the International Community School, PO Box
70282, Addis Ababa and Sandford English Community School, PO
Box 30056, Addis Ababa, the main international schools. Ethiopia has
two universities: Addis Ababa (POB 1176) and Asmara (POB 1220).
Recruitment: ECIS.

FIJI   Pop: 714,000   Area: 18,300 sq km   GNP: $1,850
High Commission: 34 Hyde Park Gate, London SW7 5BN (tel: 01-584
3661).
Ministry of Education: Suva.

Fiji, with its 300 islands and population mainly of Indian and Poly-
nesian stock, has virtually achieved universal education. The most important educational institution here is the University of the South Pacific
in Suva which serves eleven countries in the region and is staffed largely by expatriates. There are also colleges of agriculture, technology and
medicine. International schools exist at Pacific Harbour (PO Box 50)
and Suva (PO Box 2393).
Recruitment: ACU; VSO.

FINLAND   Pop: 5m   Area: 338,00 sq km   GNP: $11,000
Embassy: 38 Chesham Place, London SW1X 8HW (tel: 01-235 9531).
Ministry of Education: Rauhankatu 4, 00170 Helsinki 17.

There are approximately 700 foreign teachers in Finland in state schools, private schools, language schools, universities and Finnish-British Societies. The principal need is for TEFL teachers. Helsinki has an International School and an English School. There are universities in Helsinki, Jyväskyla, Oulu, Tampere, Joensuu, Kuopio, Lapland, Vaasa and Turku. In some cases instruction is in Swedish not Finnish!

Work permits must be obtained in advance by the prospective employer.
Recruitment: ECIS; International House; Inlingua.

FRANCE   Pop: 55.5m   Area: 544,000 sq km   GNP: $9,860
Embassy: 22 Wilton Crescent, London SW1X 8SB (tel: 01-235 8080);
    58 Knightsbridge, London SW1X 7JT.
Ministry of Education: 110 rue de Grenelle, 75700 Paris.

The country is divided into 27 educational districts called *académies* responsible for the administration of education in that particular region. For expatriate teachers without a French pedagogical qualification opportunities in state schools are available only on an exchange basis. 15% of French children attend private schools, and employment in this sector looks more encouraging. For more information consult:

● Enseignement privé catholique, 277 rue St Jacques, 75005 Paris
● Fédération de l'Enseignement Laique, 5 rue de la Santé, 75013 Paris

International schools exist in Cannes (Anglo American School, Mougins; Centre International de Valbonne); Chambon-sur-Lignon (Collège Cevenol); Nice (American International School); and Paris where there are several, including the British School, the American School and the International School. There are universities and institutes of higher education in all major cities which sometimes need TEFL staff. Private language institutes abound.
Recruitment: Central Bureau; ECIS; ELT; International House; Inlingua.

French overseas departments and territories
Ministry of Overseas Departments and Territories, 27 rue Oudinot, 75700 Paris.
Opportunities in TEFL may exist in Gudaeloupe, Guiana, Martinique — at the Université Antilles Guyane, for instance. The Université de la Réunion, 24 Avenue de la Victoire, St Denis, Réunion, might also be worth trying.

GABON   Pop: 1.3m   Area: 268,000 sq km   GNP: $4,250
Embassy: 48 Kensington Court, London W8 5DB (tel: 01-937 5285).

One of the most prosperous countries in Africa south of the Sahara thanks to abundant mineral resources and a small population, it is also one of the most advanced educationally. 70% of all children attend primary and secondary school. Half the teachers here are expatriates, mostly French nationals. The Université Omar Bongo, BP 13, Libreville might have vacancies for TEFL. A second university is planned in Franceville. A work permit, teaching certificate, medical and vaccination certificates are required for anyone wishing to work in Gabon.

GAMBIA   Pop: 700,000   Area: 11,000 sq km   GNP: $260
High Commission: 57 Kensington Court, London W8 5DG (tel: 01-937 6316).
Ministry of Education: Bedford Place Building, Banjul.

There are sixteen secondary technical, eight secondary high and nine post secondary schools in this former British enclave surrounded by Senegal. Among the institutions employing expatriates is Gambia College, which provides teacher training, agricultural courses and health training.
Recruitment: VSO.

GERMANY, DEMOCRATIC REPUBLIC OF (EAST GERMANY)
Pop: 16.5m   Area: 108,000 sq km   GNP: $9,800
Embassy: 34 Belgrave Square, London SW1X 8QB (tel: 01-235 9941).
Ministry of Education: Unter den Linden 69-73, 1086 Berlin.
Ministry of Higher and Technical Education: Marx-Engels-Platz 2, 102 Berlin.

At present there are a few officially-recruited teaching opportunities at university level.
Recruitment: British Council; Central Bureau.

GERMANY, FEDERAL REPUBLIC OF (WEST GERMANY)
Pop: 61m   Area: 249,000 sq km   GNP: $11,090
Embassy: 23 Belgrave Square, London SW1X 8PZ (tel: 01-235 5033).

There are numerous opportunities for teachers, particularly TEFL teachers in Germany both in the state system and the private system. Education is the responsibility of the federal states which make up Germany, and the state ministries of education can provide information on opportunities:
Baden Württemburg: Neues Schloss, D-7000 Stuttgart

Bayern (Bavaria): Salvatorplatz 2, D-8000 München
Berlin: Bredtschneiderstrasse 5, D-1000 Berlin 19
Bremen: Rembertiring 8-12, D-2800 Bremen 1
Hamburg: Hamburgerstrasse 31, D-2000 Hamburg 76
Hessen: Luisenplatz 10, D-6200 Wiesbaden
Niedersachsen (Lower Saxony): Schiffgraben 12, D-3000 Hanover 1
Nordrhein-Westfalen: Völkingerstrasse 49 D-4000 Düsseldorf 1
Rheinland Pfalz: Mittlere Bleiche 61, D-6500 Mainz
Saarland: Saaruferstrasse 30-32, D-6600 Saarbrücken 1
Schleswig Holstein: Düsternbrookerweg 64, D-2300 Kiel

Applications to tertiary institutions can be made direct. In addition there are opportunities in language schools, adult institutes (Volkshochschulen), companies, universities and also in the British service schools in Northern Germany. There are international schools in Berlin (John F. Kennedy School), Bonn (British, American), Düsseldorf, Frankfurt, Hamburg, Munich and Stuttgart. The Zentralstelle für Arbeitsvermittlung, Feuerbachstr 42, D-6000 Frankfurt/Main 1, recruits teachers for both the public and the private sector.

EC nationals may work in Germany for up to three months without a permit.

Recruitment: CBT; Central Bureau; ECIS: Inlingua; International House; SCEA.

GHANA   Pop: 13m   Area: 239,000 sq km   GNP: $350
High Commission: 13 Belgrave Square, London SW1X 8PR (tel: 01-235 4142).
Secretariat for Education: PO Box M45, Accra.

Ghana has three universities: University of Cape Coast; University of Ghana (Accra); University of Science and Technology (Kumasai). There are two international schools in Accra.
Recruitment: British Council; VSO; Universities of Ghana Office, 321 City Road, London EC1V 1LJ.

GIBRALTAR   Pop: 29,000   Area: 5½ sq km   GNP: $5,420
Government Office: Arundel Great Court, 179 Strand, London WC2.

The educational system amounts to twelve primary and two secondary schools. There are two primary schools for the children of service personnel and a College of FE open to all but managed by the Ministry of Defence.
Recruitment: SCEA.

GREECE   Pop: 10m   Area: 132,000 sq km   GNP: $3,740
Embassy: 1a Holland Park, London W11 3TP (tel: 01-727 8040).
Ministry of Education: 15 Mitropoleos Street, Athens.

Many private language schools and private schools employ expatriate
teachers and advertise regularly in the *Times Educational Supplement*.
There are also opportunities in TEFL at the country's thirteen univer-
sities. Among the international schools are the American Community
Schools, Athens College, Campion School (Athens) and St Catherine's
British Embassy School.
Recruitment: British Council; ECIS.

GRENADA   Pop: 110,000   Area: 344 sq km   GNP: $940
High Commission: 1 Collingham Gardens, London SW5 0HW (tel:
   01-373 7808).
Ministry of Education: St George's.

Expatriate teachers are involved in secondary education and special
education here. The main tertiary institutions are St George's University School of Medicine, a technical college, a teacher training college,
School of Agriculture (Mirabeau), School of Fishing (Victoria) and a
branch of the University of the West Indies.
Recruitment: VSO.

GUATEMALA   Pop: 7.7m   Area: 109,000 sq km
GNP: $1,120
Embassy: 13 Fawcett Street, London SW10 (tel: 01-351 3042).
Ministry of Education: Palacio Nacional, Guatemala City.

Diplomatic relations have now been restored between Britain and
Guatemala which claims Belize. The country has five universities but
its adult illiteracy rate (45%) is the second highest in the Western
hemisphere.

GUINEA   Pop: 6.4m   Area: 246,000 sq km   GNP: $300
Ministry of National Education: Conakry.

This former French possession has good mineral and agricultural potential and could become quite prosperous, but the centralised economy
of the socialist-minded government has proved inefficient. Liberalisation is now in the air, and one consequence is that private schools have
been legalised. There is an American international school at Conakry.
Educational institutions include the brand new University of Conakry
and the Polytechnique Gamal Abdul Nassar. There are also colleges
of health, administration and vocational skills. Most of these tertiary
courses have a strong practical element akin to the sandwich course

system practised in the UK.
Recruitment: British Council.

GUYANA   Pop: 950,000   Area: 215,000 sq km   GNP: $580
High Commission: 3 Palace Court, Bayswater Road, London W2 4LP
   (tel: 01-229 7684).
Ministry of Education: 21 Brickdam, Georgetown.

The High Commission acts as a point of contact for teachers wishing
to work in Guyana. There are foreign teachers at the secondary and
tertiary level particularly in maths, science and technical subjects. All
education is in the hands of the state including the University of Guyana,
PO Box 1110, Georgetown. Guyana's state controlled economy has run
into difficulties and the country has accumulated large international
debts. Attempts at liberalisation are now under way.

HAITI   Pop: 5.3m   Area: 28,000 sq km   GNP: $320
Ministry of Education: Port au Prince.

There are two international schools in this the poorest and least
developed of all the Caribbean countries: Ecole Flamboyant and the
Union School, both at Port au Prince. The address of the University
of Haiti is Box 2279, Port au Prince.

HONDURAS   Pop: 4.3m   Area: 112 sq km   GNP: $750
Embassy: 47 Manchester Street, London W1M 5PB (tel: 01-486 3880).
Ministry of Education: Comayaguela, DC.

Basic education is compulsory in this Central American republic.
Everyone who completes this stage of their education is required to teach
two illiterate adults to read and write. Opportunities may arise at international schools in La Ceiba (Mazapan School), San Pedro Sula
(Escuela Internacional Sampedrana) and Tegucigalpa (American
School). The Universidad Nacional Autonoma at Tegucigalpa is a state
institution, but there are also two new private universities at San Pedro
and Tegucigalpa.

HONG KONG   Pop: 5.5m   Area: 1,000 sq km   GNP: $6,273
Government Office: 6 Grafton Street, London W1X 3LB (tel: 01-499
   9821).
Directorate of Education: Lee Gardens 5f, 33-37 Hysan Avenue,
   Causeway Bay, Hong Kong.

The Government Office publishes a useful fact sheet on living conditions
in Hong Kong.

Education in Hong Kong is free and compulsory up to the age of 15. There are three types of school: government schools, schools run by voluntary bodies (usually the churches) which receive government assistance, and private independent schools. In addition there is a small group of English schools for English-speaking children, notably the twelve schools operated by the English Schools Foundation. The Government has an ambitious programme to improve the standard of English and in 1987 the British Council recruited a sizeable number of teachers for the state sector.

The Vocational Training Council operates eight technical institutes, and there are four teacher training colleges: Grantham, Northcote, Sir Robert Black, and the Hong Kong Technical Teachers' College. There are currently five tertiary level institutions: University of Hong Kong, the Chinese University of Hong Kong, the Hong Kong Polytechnic, the City Polytechnic of Hong Kong and the Hong Kong Baptist College.

Useful addresses in Hong Kong:

English Schools Foundation, GPO Box 11284

HK International School, South Bay Close, Repulse Bay (American style)

Chinese International School, 7 Eastern Hospital Road, Causeway Bay

Kellet School, 2 Wak Lok Path, Wah Fu Estate

Sir Ellis Kadoorie School, 9 Eastern Hospital Road, Sookunpo (Govt school)

British citizens planning to work in Hong Kong are now required to obtain a visa from the British Passport Office or a British Consulate prior to their arrival.

Recruitment: ACU; British Council; ECIS; SCEA.

HUNGARY   Pop: 10.6m   Area: 93,000 sq km   GNP: $2,050
Embassy: 35 Eaton Place, London SW1X 8BY (tel: 01-235 2664).
Ministry of Education: Szalayu U 10/14, 1055 Budapest.

Hungary has been one of the more liberal countries in Eastern Europe in recent years and, unlike its neighbours, offers opportunities in government schools, private schools, universities and language schools teaching EFL, science, maths and technical subjects. The Government has set up two bilingual Hungarian/English schools. There is an American School in Budapest. Your employer must register you with the police on arrival. Currency cannot be taken out of the country, but part of a contract teacher's salary is usually paid in hard currency.

Recruitment: British Council; Central Bureau; International House.

ICELAND   Pop: 239,000   Area: 103,000 sq km
GNP: $9,380
Embassy: 1 Eaton Terrace, London SW1W 8EY (tel: 01-730 5131/2).
Ministry of Education: Hverfisgata 4-6, 150 Reykyavik.

The University of Iceland employs a few expatriates and plans to start
a Language Institute there. The American Embassy has a school. Work
permits must be applied for in advance by the prospective employer.

INDIA   Pop: 770m   Area: 3.3m sq km   GNP: $260
High Commission: India House, Aldwych, London WC2B 4NA (tel:
    01-836 8484).

Public education is the responsibility of the state governments, and the
education departments are to be found in the following state capitals:
Aizawl, Kohima, Bhunabaneswar, Paipur, Gantok, Madras, Agartala,
Lucknow, Calcutta, Simla, Srinagar, Bangalore, Trivandrum, Bhopal,
Bombay, Imphal, Shillong, Hyderabad, Itangar, Dispur, Patna,
Ganhinagar, Chandigarh.
    Private education, including church schools, exists alongside the state
sector. However, India is self-sufficient in teachers, and it is increas-
ingly difficult for a foreigner to obtain a work permit. This is less of
a problem when it comes to international schools: Bangalore (ADITI,
International), Bombay (American, International), Calcutta,
Hyderabad, Mussoorie (International, Woodstock), New Delhi
(American Embassy School, British School), Ootacamund (Hebron
School) and Tamil Nadu (Kodaikanal International).
    India has some 135 universities and about 10,000 affiliated colleges.

INDONESIA   Pop: 165m   Area: 1.9m sq km   GNP: $540
Embassy: 10 Portman Street, London W1 9AQ.
Visa Section: 157 Edgware Road, London W2 2HR (tel: 01-499 7661).
Education & Cultural Attaché: 10 Portman Street, London W1 9AQ.
Ministry of Education: Jalan Jenderal Sudirman, Senayan, Jakarta
    Pusat.

There are international schools at Balikpapan, Bandung (two), Bogor,
Bontang, Jakarta (two), Malang, Medan (two), Salatiga, Semarang,
Sentani, Serukam, Sumatra, Surabaya and Tembagapura. The British
Council has a DTO in Jakarta and there are a large number of private
language schools. There are both state and private universities, and there
are also opportunities in teacher training and with oil companies.
Recruitment: British Council; ECIS; VSO.

IRAN   Pop: 45m   Area: 1.65m sq km   GNP: $2,160
Embassy: 27 Prince's Gate, London SW7 1PX (tel: 01-584 8101).
Consulate: 50 Kensington Court, London W8 5DD (tel: 01-937 5225).
Ministry of Education: Teheran.

Although there appear to be no openings in Iran at present, the future looks more promising now that the conflict with Iraq is over.

IRAQ   Pop: 16m   Area: 435,000 sq km   GNP: $3,020
Embassy: 22 Queen's Gate, London SW7 5JG (tel: 01-584 7141).
Ministry of Education: PO Box 258, Baghdad.

Baghdad International School is the only private school in the country, and there are no European teachers in state schools. There are six universities including two in Baghdad, one in Mosul and one at Basra where some postgraduate courses are taught through the medium of English. The number of teaching opportunities is likely to grow as the country returns to normality following the cessation of hostilities with Iran.
Recruitment: British Council.

ISRAEL   Pop: 4m   Area: 21,000 sq km   GNP: $5,100
Embassy: 2 Palace Green, London W8 4QB (tel: 01-937 8050).
Ministry of Education: Hakirya, 14 Klausner Street, Tel Aviv.

Generally speaking, Israel is self-sufficient in teachers. Even all the staff at the British Council's DTO are locally recruited. There may, however, be opportunities at the three international schools: The Anglican School, PO Box 191, Jerusalem; England Israel High School, Kfar Hanoar Hadatoi, Kfar Hasidim 20494; Walworth Barbour American International School, Rehov Hazorea, Kfar Shmaryahu, Tel Aviv.

There are very few private language schools since the district authorities usually fulfil this need. At the tertiary level there is the Israel Institute of Technology (Haifa), Hebrew University of Jerusalem, Bar-Ilan University, Tel Aviv University, Haifa University, Ben-Gurion University of the Negev.
Further Reading: Mark Taylor: *Education in the Service of the State of Israel* (Anglo-Israel Association, 9 Bentinck Street, London W1M 5RP).
Recruitment: ECIS.

ITALY   Pop: 57m   Area: 301,000 sq km   GNP: $7,000
Embassy: 14 Three Kings Yard, Davies Street, London W1Y 2EH (tel: 01-629 8200).

Consulates: 38 Eaton Place, London W1; 111 Piccadilly, Manchester 2; 7-9 Greyfriars, Bedford MK40 1HJ.
Italian Institute: 39 Belgrave Square, London SW1X 8NX.
Ministry of Education: Viale Trastevere 76A, 00100 Rome.

There are no opportunities in state schools except under an exchange scheme though there may be opportunities in the private sector. There are international schools in Florence, Genoa, Imperia (Liceo Internazionale), Milan (American, International, Sir James Henderson), Naples, Rome (Ambrit, American Overseas, Castelli, Greenwood Garden, International Academy, Kendale Primary, Marymount, New, Notre Dame International, Southlands, St George's, St Stephen's, Summerfield), Trieste (International, UWC), Turin, Varese (EC School) and Venice.

Language schools abound, some affiliated to an international group, others to an Italian organisation, such as the British School Group which alone has 74 branches (British School Group, Vilae Liegei 14, 00198, Roma; British College, Via Luigi Rizzo 18, 95131 Catania). The British Council has institutes in Italy, too. There could also be opportunities in Italy's many universities.

EC employment conditions apply. If you find work in Italy you should obtain a *Libretto di Lavoro* from the Town Hall and then obtain a *Carta di soggiorno di cittaddino di uno Stato membro della CEE.* The Italian Embassy issues a booklet on employment in Italy.
Recruitment: British Council; Canning; Central Bureau; ECIS; ELT; International House; Inlingua.

IVORY COAST (CÔTE D'IVOIRE) Pop: 10.6m Area: 322,000 sq km
GNP: $720
Embassy: 2 Upper Belgrave Street, London SW1X 8BJ (tel: 01-235 6991).
Ministry of Education: BP V120, Abidjan.

This used to be one of the most prosperous countries in the whole of Africa, but the collapse of world prices for timber, cocoa, and coffee (the Ivory Coast's main resources) reduced the per capita GNP by almost half. Nevertheless, the proportion of children in primary school remains relatively high (80%), and the Government has invested in five new technical training institutes. The National University of the Ivory Coast is at Abidjan. There are international schools at Abidjan, Kingston (Priory School), and Mandeville (Belair School).
Recruitment: British Council; ECIS; OMOCI (Office de la Main d'Oeuvre en Côte d'Ivoire, BP 108, Abidjan).

JAMAICA   Pop: 2.2m   Area: 11,000 sq km   GNP: $1,080
High Commission: 63 St James's Street, London SW1A 1LY (tel: 01-629 5477).
Ministry of Education: 2 National Heroes Circle, Kingston 4.

Opportunities might arise at the tertiary level institutions: College of Arts, Science and Technology; School of Agriculture; University of the West Indies (Mona Campus).

JAPAN   Pop: 121m   Area: 378,000 sq km   GNP: $10,390
Embassy: 46 Grosvenor Street, London W1X 0BA (tel: 01-493 6030).
Ministry of Education: 3-2 Kasumigaseki, Chiyoda-ku, Tokyo.

The Japanese authorities are keen to promote international contacts, and the Ministry of Education administers a scheme known as the Japan Exchange and Teaching Programme (JET). This is open to the nationals of most English-speaking countries and the agents in the UK are Gabbitas, Truman & Thring. The scheme is limited to under 35s, and would suit an unattached person from university. Teaching qualifications, though desirable, are not obligatory. What is required, however, is an interest in TEFL and Japan. Most teachers are based in schools, but some may be assigned to the local education inspectorate.

Japan has become a Mecca for foreign businessmen these days and as a consequence there are a good many international schools. Salaries tend to be high, but so is the cost of living. There are international schools in Fukuoka, Hiroshima, Kobe (three), Kyoto, Nagoya, Okinawa (two), Sapporo, Tokyo (nine), Yokohama (three). Most of the 400 or so private language schools are Japanese-owned and may have an American link. The British Council has set up a wholly-owned DTO in Kyoto, while in Tokyo they have gone into partnership with a Japanese firm to run the Cambridge School of English. Opportunities exist, especially for TEFL teachers, in both the state and private universities. At one time many such posts offered security of tenure, but now universities only offer short term contracts.

Reference book: Directory of English Studies in Japan (British Council, Tokyo).

Recruitment: British Council; Canning; ECIS; ILC; Japan Recruitment Queen's English Language Schools.

JORDAN   Pop: 3.5m   Area: 98,000 sq km   GNP: $1,900
Embassy: 6 Upper Phillimore Gardens, London W8 7HB (tel: 01-937 3685).
Ministry of Education: PO Box 1646, Amman.

There are three English medium international schools in Amman: the American Community School; the Amman Bacclaureate School; the International Community School. English is the medium of instruction in the upper classes of some private secondary schools. Apart from the state and private sectors of education, there is education provision for Palestinian refugees by UNRWA, PO Box 484, Amman. Jordan has three universities: University of Jordan (Amman); Yarmouk and Mo'ata. TEFL is the subject most in demand.
Recruitment: British Council; ECIS.

KENYA   Pop: 20m   Area: 583,000 sq km   GNP: $300
High Commission: 24/25 New Bond Street, London W1Y 9HD (tel: 01-636 2371/5).
Ministry of Education: PO Box 30040, Nairobi.

The educational system comprises both government and government-assisted schools. There are a number of international schools, including the International School and St Mary's School (both in Nairobi) which prepare pupils for the International Baccalaureate. Apart from the Universities of Nairobi and Moi (the latter completed in 1989), there are three Polytechnics (Mombasa, Kenya and Eldoret), as well as the Jomo Kenyatta University of Agriculture and Technology.
Recruitment: British Council; ECIS; ODA; VSO.

KIRIBATI   Pop: 62,000   Area: 861 sq km   GNP: $460
Ministry of Education: PO Box 263, Bikenibeu, Tarawa.

Kiribati's 33 atolls are scattered over 5m sq km of sea, yet every inhabited atoll has at least one primary school. There is a Marine Training School at Tarawa and a Technical Institute at Betio.
Recruitment: British Council; Christians Abroad; VSO.

KOREA, DEMOCRATIC PEOPLE'S REPUBLIC OF (NORTH KOREA)   Pop: 20m   Area: 121,000 sq km   GNP: $1,170
Ministry of Education: Pyongyang.

Until recently North Korea was strongly xenophobic. Now the country is trying to develop relations with the outside world, so there has been some relaxation. Whether that means there will be opportunities for expatriate teachers remains to be seen. English is a compulsory second language from the age of 14 onwards. If opportunities occur they are likely to be in the TEFL field, notably in the one university (at Pyongyang) or the 170 other tertiary institutions.

KOREA, REPUBLIC OF (SOUTH KOREA)   Pop: 42m
Area: 99,000 sq km   GNP: $2,032
Embassy: 4 Palace Gate, London W8 5NF (tel: 01-581 0247).
Ministry of Education: 77-6 Sejong-no, Chongno-ku, Seoul.

A country which has made rapid strides forward on the economic front and is now seen as a second Japan. The education system is well developed, and strongly influenced by the US, with good opportunities for any teachers willing to seek them out. There are three international schools in Seoul (British, Foreign, International) and one in Taejon (Korea Christian Academy). Opportunities exist for TEFL teachers at the Sogang University Language Institute, Korea Herald Language Training Centre, Sisa Young-Ho-Sa, and numerous other language institutes. The country boasts some 98 universities.
Recruitment: ELT.

KUWAIT   Pop: 1.6m   Area: 18,000 sq km   GNP: $15,410
Embassy: 45-46 Queen's Gate, London SW7 (tel: 01-589 4533).
Ministry of Education: PO Box 7, Safat, Hilali Street.

An oil state for three decades which has spent much of its wealth on creating efficient social services and a good educational system. However, education, though free, does not appear to be universal. There are international schools at Fahaheel (The English School), Jabriya (New English School, Al-Bayan School — the latter bilingual English/Arabic), Khaldiya (Universal American School), Safat (Sunshine School), Salmiya (Kuwait English School), Salwa (American School, Gulf English School), Surra (The English School), Yarmuk (Modern School). Expatriates are also employed in language schools, such as the Pitman School, and in tertiary institutions: University of Kuwait; Teacher Training Institute; Commercial Institute; Institute of Applied Technology; Clinical Institute. The social system is highly conservative, and expatriates must take care not to offend local sensibilities. The consumption of alcohol is foribidden by law.

LAOS   Pop: 3.7m   Area: 237,000 sq km   GNP: $80
Ministry of Education: Vientiane.

Since 1975 Laos has adopted a policy of isolationism, and teachers from the West are unlikely to be allowed in. The educational system used to follow the French pattern, but now has a strong Socialist content. There is a university in Vientiane: Sisavangvong University.

LEBANON   Pop: 2.7m   Area: 10,400 sq km   GNP: $1070
Embassy: 21 Kensington Palace Gardens, London W8 4QM (tel: 01-229
    7265).
Ministry of Education: Beirut.

Formerly regarded as the cultural centre of the Arab world with the
highest literacy rate, Lebanon is currently in turmoil. It is inadvisable
to visit, let alone take up employment there until peace returns. Many
organisations which used to employ foreign teachers, such as the
American University of Beirut, no longer do so, though the University's New York office (850 Third Avenue, 18th Floor, New York, NY
10022) still recruits staff (but not US passport holders). The Embassy
will be able to provide an up-to-date picture.

LESOTHO   Pop: 1.5m   Area: 30,000 sq km   GNP: $470
High Commission: 10 Collingham Road, London SW5 0NR (tel: 01-373
    8581).
Ministry of Education: PO Box 47, Maseru 100.

This landlocked country is surrounded by South Africa and enjoys a
mild climate. It has a high level of literacy, with much of the education
being provided by mission schools (Evangelical, Roman Catholic and
Anglican). There are international schools at Mafeteng (Kingsgate High
School), Maseru (Machabeng High School and Maseru English Medium
Preparatory School). The National University of Lesotho at Roma
(which once formed part of the University of Botswana) has an international primary school taking children till the age of 13.
Recruitment: British Council; ECIS; IVS; ODA.

MADAGASCAR   Pop: 10m   Area: 587,000 sq km
GNP: $270
Honorary Consulate: 69-70 Mark Lane, London EC3R 7JA.
Nearest Embassy: 4 Avenue Raphael, 75016 Paris.
Ministry of Secondary and Basic Education: Anosy, Antananarivo.
Ministry of Higher Education: Tsimbazaza, Antananarivo.

The fourth largest island in the world received its independence from
France in 1960. The educational system is basically French but the
Malagasy language is being promoted these days. There are two
American schools here at Antananarivo and Antsirabe. There is also
a university with six regional centres.

MALAWI   Pop: 7.3m   Area: 118,500 sq km   GNP: $210
High Commission: 33 Grosvenor Street, London W1X 0DE (tel: 01-491
    4972).

Ministry of Education: Private Bag 328, Capital City, Lilongwe 3.

About 100 foreign teachers work at schools in the public sector, including the prestigious Kamazu Academy for high-fliers, the 'Eton of Africa'. There is a particular demand for teachers of maths, science and technical subjects. The Embassy handles recruitment for technical schools. On arrival in the country the Ministry of Education arranges a six-week induction course for new teachers. Up to two-thirds of net earnings can be remitted out of the country. There are international schools at Blantyre (St Andrew's), Lilongwe (Bishop Mackenzie), Libe (Hillview Primary), Zomba (Sir Harry Johnston Primary). Among the tertiary level institutions are the University of Malawi, Chancellor College, Malawi Polytechnic, Bonda College and the Kamazu School of Nursing.
Recruitment: British Council; Christians Abroad; VSO.

MALAYSIA   Pop: 15.7m   Area: 330,000 sq km
GNP: $2,000
High Commission: 45 Belgrave Square, London SW1X 8QT (tel: 01-491 4172).
Ministry of Education: 9th-25th Floors, Bangunan Bank Pertanian, Leboh Pasar Besar, 50604 Kuala Lumpur.

Malaysia, consisting of mainland Malaya, Sarawak and Sabah, is a comparatively prosperous country. It is racially very mixed with Malays, Chinese, Indians and Dayeks. CBT recruits TEFL teachers mainly for the secondary sector. The British Council has its own language institute in Kuala Lumpur. There are international schools in the Cameroon Highlands (Chefoo School), Kota Kinabalu (International), Kuala Lumpur (Garden International, International) and Penang (Dalat, St Christopher's, Uplands). The country boasts seven universities, four polytechnics and 21 teacher training colleges. In addition there is a regional centre for science and mathematics teaching (RECSAM) in Penang.
Recruitment: British Council; CBT.

MALI   Pop: 8.2m   Area: 1.24m sq km   GNP: $150
Ministry of National Education: BP 71, Bamako.

An extremely poor country with only 25% receiving a basic education. With assistance from agencies such as the World Bank and UNDP there is a drive to make education more vocationally orientated. Great emphasis is being put on agricultural training and functional literacy programmes. There are five tertiary level institutions and an institute of

higher studies using French as the teaching medium. There is an American International School in Bamako.
Recruitment: British Council.

MALTA   Pop: 350,000   Area: 316 sq km   GNP: $3,370
High Commission: 16 Kensington Square, London W8 5HH (tel: 01-938 1712).
Ministry of Education: Lascaris, Valletta.

Malta's substantial private education sector includes 80 Roman Catholic schools. International schools are St Edward's College and Verdala School, both in Cottonera. Malta also has a university.

MAURITANIA   Pop: 1.5m   Area: 1m sq km   GNP: $440
Ministry of Education: BP 183, Nouakchott.

With one of the lowest literacy rates in Africa (17%) and a largely nomadic population, Mauritania is struggling to improve its educational standards. There is an American International School at Nouakchott, and at the tertiary level there is the University of Nouakchott, the Ecole Nationale des Sciences, and the Ecole Nationale d'Administration.

MAURITIUS   Pop: 1m   Area: 2,000 sq km   GNP: $1,150
High Commission: 32 Elvaston Place, London SW7 5NW (tel: 01-581 0294).
Ministry of Education: New Government Centre, Port Louis.

This Indian Ocean island with high educational standards (over 80% literacy) appears to be largely self-sufficient in teachers. There is an international school, Alexandra House, in Vacoas. At the tertiary level there is the University of Mauritius, Mauritius Institute of Education, and the Mahatma Gandhi Institute.

MEXICO   Pop: 81m   Area: 1.97m sq km   GNP: $2,200
Embassy: 60 Trafalgar Square, London SW1 (tel: 01-235 6393).
Consulate: 8 Halkin Street, London SW1X 7DW.
Ministry of Education: República de Argentina y Gonzales Obrégon 28, 06029 Mexico, DF.

Mexico currently suffers from high inflation and a large international debt problem. A strongly nationalistic country, it has universal education at the primary level, as well as a high enrolment in secondary schools. There are American international schools in Durango, Guadalajara, Mexico City, Monterrey (two), Pachuca, Puebla, Queretaro and Torreon. Also in Mexico City are El Colegio Britanico

and Greengates School. Among the language schools operating are those of the Anglo-Mexican Cultural Institute. There are a large number of universities which follow the American academic pattern, the most important being the Universidad Autónoma de México in Mexico City.
Recruitment: British Council.

MONGOLIA   Pop: 1.82m   Area: 1.6m sq km   GNP: $700
Embassy: 7 Kensington Court, London W8 5DL (tel: 01-937 5238).
Ministry of Education: Ulan Bator.

This central Asian republic has a developed educational system which includes one university and seven other higher education institutions.
Recruitment: British Council.

MOROCCO   Pop: 21m   Area: 447,000 sq km   GNP: $670
Embassy: 49 Queen's Gate Gardens, London SW7 5NE (tel: 01-581 5001).
Ministry of Education: Quartier des Ministères, Rabat.

Education follows the French model and the teachers are nowadays largely Moroccan. However, there are still opportunities in the state system for foreigners. American international schools flourish at Casablanca, Rabat and Tangier. The British Council has a language institute in Rabat, and there are a few commercial private schools of English, such as the International Language Centre, Rabat; the Tutor Centre, Agadir; and the English Institute, Casablanca. There are universities at Rabat, Fez, Casablanca (two), Kenitra, Marrakesh, Oudja, Meknes, Tetnan and El Jadida.
Recruitment: British Council; Central Bureau; International House.

MOZAMBIQUE   Pop: 13.5m   Area: 801,590 sq km   GNP: $150
Embassy: 159 New Bond Street, London W1Y 9PA (tel: 01-493 0694).
Ministry of Education: Avda 24 de Julho 167, Maputo.

This former Portuguese colony is beset by civil war at the moment, which has set back the Government's efforts to improve education. Numbers attending school have fallen in recent years. Tertiary level education is provided by the Eduardo Mondlane University, Maputo.
Recruitment: IVS.

NEPAL   Pop: 17m   Area: 141,000 sq km   GNP: $170
Embassy: 12a Kensington Gardens, London W8 4QU (tel: 01-229 6231).
Ministry of Education: Kathmandu.

There are a number of opportunities for foreign teachers in this Himalayan kingdom. The British Government is supporting the Budhanilkantha School and there are also foreign lecturers at Tribhuvan University and the Campus of International Languages. VSO are involved with a UNICEF women's education project. Expatriate education is provided by the British Primary School and the Lincoln School in Kathmandu.

Recruitment: British Council; VSO; ECIS.

NETHERLANDS   Pop: 14.5m   Area: 41,000 sq km   GNP: $9,430
Embassy: 28 Hyde Park Gate, London SW7 5DP (tel: 01-584 5040).
Ministry of Education: Post Bus 25000, 2700 LZ Zoetermeer.

Foreign teachers not in possession of a Dutch qualification may have permission to teach as an unqualified teacher at the secondary level, but the employing school has to apply to the Inspector of Education for approval. The Foreign Countries and Minorities Branch (Information Division), Ministry of Education, Post Bus 25000, 2700 LZ Zoetermeer, can provide further information. Vacancies are often advertised in *Het Weekblad voor Leraren bij het VWO en HAVO* the weekly journal for secondary school teachers (c/o Intermedia BV, Postbus 371, 2400 AJ Alphen aan de Rijn).

The Netherlands has a large number of international schools including the EC School at Bergen, British Schools in Amsterdam and The Hague, and others in Amsterdam, Arnhem, Brunssum, Eindhoven, Groningen, Hilversum, Leiden, Maastricht, Ommen, Rotterdam, Vilsteren and Werkhoven. There are universities at Leiden, Utrecht, Groningen, Limburg, Rotterdam (Erasmus), Amsterdam (University of Amsterdam and Free University of Amsterdam), Nijmegen (Catholic University).

EC nationals should contact the local police for a residence permit within a week of their arrival if they intend to work for more than three months.

Recruitment: British Council; DES; ECIS.

NEW ZEALAND   Pop: 3.2m   Area: 269,000 sq km   GNP: $7,240
High Commission: New Zealand House, Haymarket, London SW1Y 4TQ (tel: 01-930 8422).
Department of Education: Private Bag, Wellington.

New Zealand is currently suffering from a slight shortage of teachers, although there are no opportunities for foreign teachers in primary schools. A teacher exchange scheme is in operation and, in addition, immigration applications can be considered from teachers who have obtained a firm guarantee of employment from a secondary school (state or private) in New Zealand. All applications are assessed in consultation with the Ministry of Education. For information on opportunities in the private sector contact: Association of Heads of Independent Secondary Schools of NZ (Incorp), PO Box 5028, Greenmeadows, Hawkes Bay.

Tertiary level lecturers (apart from junior staff) figure on the Occupational Priority list. There are six universities (Auckland, Hamilton, Palmerston North, Wellington, Christchurch and Dunedin); 22 technical universities or community colleges, and six teachers' colleges. Advertisements sometimes appear in the *Times Higher Education Supplement*.

Recruitment: ACU; League for the Exchange of Commonwealth Teachers.

NICARAGUA   Pop: 3m   Area: 130,000 sq km   GNP: $960
Embassy: 8 Gloucester Road, London SW7 4PP (tel: 01-584 3231).
Ministry of Education: Apdo 108, Managua, JR.

There are opportunities for volunteer teachers in this beautiful but troubled Central American state. Helen Yuill, Nicaragua Solidarity Campaign, 23 Bevenden Street, London N1 6BH (tel: 01-253 2464) can provide full details. In Managua there is an American-Nicaraguan School, and the country boasts four universities.

In order to get a visa the employing organisation must apply to the Ministry of External Co-operation for a technical visa to be issued by the Nicaraguan Embassy.

Recruitment: CIIR; Nicaragua Solidarity Campaign.

NIGER   Pop: 5.7m   Area: 1.3m sq km   GNP: $240.
Ministry of Education: Niamey.

The World Bank is involved in a number of educational projects in Niger and the British Council provides an adviser to the Ministry of Education. There is an American school in Niamey. Opportunities could exist at the University of Niamey.

Recruitment: British Council.

NIGERIA: 99m   Area: 924,000 sq km   GNP: $770
High Commission: Nigeria House, 9 Northumberland Avenue, London WC2N 5BX (tel: 01-839 1244); *Education Division:* 180 Tottenham Court Road, London W1P 9LE.
Ministry of Education: 3 Moloney Street, Lagos.

Nigeria has an extensive educational system but, because of expansion in the tertiary sector, is by no means self-sufficient in teachers. There are international schools in Ibadan, Jos, Kaduna and Lagos (three). Nigeria has 24 universities and their recruitment is handled in the UK by the Nigerian Universities Office in the Education Division of the High Commission.
Recruitment: British Council; ECIS.

NORWAY   Pop: 4.2m   Area: 324,000 sq km   GNP: $13,700
Embassy: 25 Belgrave Square, London SW1X 8QD (tel: 01-235 7151).
Ministry of Education: PO Box 8119, 0032 Oslo.

It is not easy for a foreign teacher to find a full-time post in the schools system, since knowledge of Norwegian is required. Moreover, the country appears to be more than self-sufficient in teachers. Teaching appointments are made by the local school board (*skolestyre*) in the case of schools dealing with the 7-16 age group. The regional school board (*fylkesskolestyre*) appoints teachers at the upper secondary level. Tertiary institutions handle their own recruitment.

There are international schools in Bergen, Oslo (American School, British School), Stavanger (American School, British School) and Trondheim (Birralee). TEFL teachers can find employment with language schools and two voluntary adult education organisations: Studenteramfundets Friundervisning, Nedre vollgt 20, Oslo 1; Arbeidernes Opplysningsforbund, Storgt. 23d, Oslo 1. Vacancies in Norwegian schools and colleges are advertised in *Norsk Lysingsblat* (Akersgt. 34, Oslo 1 — subscription 91 Norwegian kroner per quarter).
Recruitment: British Council; Inlingua; ECIS.

OMAN   Pop: 2m   Area: 213,000 sq km   GNP: $6,300
Embassy: 44A Montpelier Square, London SW7 1JJ (tel: 01-584 6782).
Ministry of Education: Ruwi.

Since the early seventies vast sums have been invested in the modernisation of the country, including education. There is a strong British influence here. A large number of instructors and TEFL teachers work with the armed forces, and there are several private language institutes in the main cities. Most of the positions are bachelor status. Education for expatriates is provided by the Muscat English Speaking School at Ruwi, while the Sultan's School at Seeb provides a bilingual education largely for Arab pupils. At the tertiary level there is a teacher training institute and a university has opened recently.
Recruitment: Airwork; British Council; ECIS; International House; ILC.

PAKISTAN   Pop: 96m   Area: 796,000 sq km   GNP: $400
Embassy: 35 Lowndes Square, London SW1X 9JN (tel: 01-235 2044).
Ministry of Education: Block D, Pakistan Secretariat, Islamabad.

Pakistan is more or less self-sufficient in teachers, but opportunities
for expatriates do exist in private schools run along British public school
lines. There are international schools for the full age range at Islamabad,
Karachi (American Society School), Lahore (American Society School)
and Murree (Christian School). There is a British Primary School in
Karachi. There are universities in all the major cities including the new
private Lahore University of Management Sciences which employs
expatriates.
Recruitment: British Council; VSO.

PANAMA   Pop: 2.2m   Area: 77,000 sq km   GNP: $2,160
Embassy: 109 Jermyn Street, London SW1 (tel: 01-930 1591).
Ministry of Education: Apdo 2440, Panamá 3.

This small American state enjoys good educational standards. There
are international schools in Balboa, Colon and Puerta Arumelles
(Escuela Las Palmas). The state has three universities.
Recruitment: ECIS.

PAPUA NEW GUINEA   Pop: 3.4m   Area: 462,000 sq km
GNP: $760
High Commission: 14 Waterloo Place, London SW1R 4AR (tel: 01-930
    0922).
Ministry of Education: PSA Haus, Independence Drive, Waigani.

There is still a strong Australian influence in PNG, and Australia still
contributes a generous amount of aid. The educational system is well
developed in the main centre, less so in the remote rural areas. The
International Education Agency of PNG operates international schools
including two secondary schools at Port Moresby and Lae. At the tertiary level there is the University of Papua New Guinea and the Papua
New Guinea University of Technology.
Recruitment: ACU; ECIS; VMM; VSO.

PARAGUAY   Pop: 3.6m   Area: 406,000 sq km
GNP: $1,250
Embassy: Braemar Lodge, Cornwall Gardens, London SW7 4AQ (tel:
    01-937 1253).
Ministry of Education: Chilé, Humanitá y Piribebuy, Asunción.

There are international schools in Asunción (American School, Christian Academy). Paraguay has two universities: the National Univer-

sity and the Catholic University, both in Asunción.
Recruitment: British Council; Central Bureau.

PERU   Pop: 20m   Area: 1.3m sq km   GNP: $1,000
Embassy: 52 Sloane Street, London SW1X 9SP (tel: 01-235 6867).
Ministry of Education: Parque Universitario s/n, Lima.

Among the international schools are the Colegio Anglo-American
Prescott, Arequipa; the Southern Peru Staff Schools, Ilo; the American
School and the Sanata Margarita School, Markham College, Lima. The
British Peruvian Cultural Institute tends to recruit its TEFL teachers
locally. American Bi-national Centres teach English in nine cities and
there are a number of private language institutes. At the tertiary level
Peru has 25 state universities and ten private universities.

There are stringent labour laws governing expatriates, but there have
been several instances of globe-trotters landing temporary jobs. Salaries
tend to be low.
Recruitment: British Council; Central Bureau.

THE PHILIPPINES   Pop: 56m   Area: 300,000 sq km   GNP:
$660
Embassy: 9a Palace Green, London W8 4QE (tel: 01-937 1609).
Consular Section: 1 Cumberland House, Kensington High Street,
     London W8.
Ministry of Education: Palacio del Gobernador, General Luna Street,
     cnr Aduanda Street, Intramuros, Manila.

There is a strong American influence on the educational system, with
instruction in English and Filipino right from the primary stage. International schools exist in Baguio City, Cebu City, Makati (Faith College), and Manila (British School, Casa Montessori Internationale, International School). English is widely spoken in the Philippines and
as a consequence there are virtually no private language schools. Opportunities may exist in the University of the Philippines or the 52 other
private and state universities.
Recruitment: ECIS; VSO.

POLAND   Pop: 37m   Area: 313,000 sq km   GNP: $3,900
Embassy: 47 Portland Place, London W1N 3AG (tel: 01-580 5481).
Cultural Institute: 34 Portland Place, London W1N 4HQ (tel: 01-636
     6032).
Ministry of Education: 00-918 Warsaw, Al. I Armii WP 25.

There is an American School in Warsaw. Poland has eleven universities and eighteen technical universities and the British Council recruits

for some of them. International House expects to have an affiliated language school in operation soon in Poznan.
Recruitment: British Council; ECIS; International House.

PORTUGAL   Pop: 10m   Area: 92,000 sq km   GNP: $2,200
Embassy: 11 Belgrave Square, London SW1X 8PP (tel: 01-235 5331).
Consulate: 62 Brompton Road, London SW3 1BJ (tel: 01-581 8722).
Ministry of Education: Av 5 de Outubro 107, 1000 Lisboa.

Portugal has a number of international schools on the Algarve (International School, Colegio Internacional de Vilamoura); in Lisbon (AIS, St Anthony's, St Dominic's, St George's School, St Julian's School); in Loulé (Prince Henry); in Oporto (British). There are also a few schools with only a primary section. The main TEFL opportunities would appear to be in the language school sector. The British Council has its own teaching operation in Lisbon and Coimbra and the British Institute in Oporto has a British Council connection. Among the private languages institutes are the Cambridge School and the Central School of Languages. Among the tertiary level institutions are the Universities of Coimbra (established 1290), Porto, Aveiro, Minho, Evora, Azores and five universities in Lisbon (Technical, Catholic, New University, Free University, University of Lisbon).
Recruitment: British Council; ECIS; International House.

QATAR   Pop: 250,000   Area: 11,000 sq km   GNP: $20,600
Embassy: 27 Chesham Place, London SW1X 8HG (tel: 01-235 0851).
Consular Section: 115 Queen's Gate, London SW7 5LP.
Ministry of Education: Doha.

There are plenty of opportunities, principally for TEFL teachers, in this small oil state, where only one fifth of the population is actually Qatari. Expatriates (both Arab and European) teach at the secondary level, at the Language Teaching Institute, the Higher Teacher Training College and the University of Qatar. The Doha College for English Speaking Students (PO Box 7506) is an international secondary school. There are two primary schools for expatriates — the English Speaking School and the Independent School, both in Doha.
Recruitment: British Council.

ROMANIA   Pop: 23m   Area: 237,500 sq km   GNP: $2,540
Embassy: 4 Palace Green, London W8 4QD (tel: 01-937 9666).
Ministry of Education: Bucharest, Skr. Nuferilor 30.

As with other eastern bloc countries recruitment is done through official channels only. There is a small American School in Bucharest.

There are usually a few vacancies for English lecturers at university level. Romania has universities at Iasi, Bucharest, Cluj, Timisora, Craiova, and Brasov.
Recruitment: British Council.

RWANDA   Pop: 6m   Area: 26,000 sq km   GNP: $270
Ministry of Primary and Secondary Education: BP 622, Kigali.
Ministry of Higher Education: BP 624, Kigali.

French is the medium of instruction in this former Belgian trust territory which, in view of its position between Francophone and Anglophone countries, is keen to develop English teaching. The World Bank is assisting with the expansion of primary education. At the tertiary level the National University of Rwanda has campuses at Butari and Ruhengeri. Other tertiary institutions are the Institut Pédagogique, the Grand Seminaire, and the Ecole Supérieur Militaire.
Recruitment: Rwanda Mission.

ST. HELENA   Pop: 5,000   Area: 300 sq km
(Dependencies: Ascension — pop: 800, and Tristan da Cunha — pop: 300)

The island of St. Helena boasts eight primary schools, three senior schools and one selective secondary school, and has 71 full-time teachers. On Ascension there are local schools as well as one run by Cable and Wireless for the children of its expatriate employees. Tristan de Cunha provides schooling for around 70 children. St. Helena and Tristan de Cunha are somewhat isolated, having no airlink with the outside world.
Recruitment: ODA.

ST. LUCIA   Pop: 137,000   Area: 616 sq km   GNP: $1,390
High Commission: 10 Kensington Court, London W8 5DL (tel: 01-937 9522).
Ministry of Education: Castries.

At Morne Fortune there is a further education college and also a branch of the University of the West Indies.
Recruitment: VSO.

ST. VINCENT & THE GRENADINES   Pop: 128,000
Area: 388 sq km   GNP: $900
High Commission: 10 Kensington Court, London W8 5DL (tel: 01-937 9522).
Ministry of Education: Kingstown.

Most of the secondary schools are run by religious organisations with government assistance. St. Vincent has a technical college and a teacher training college.
Recruitment: VSO.

SAUDI ARABIA   Pop: 11m   Area: 2.15m sq km
GNP: $10,740
Embassy: 30 Belgrave Square, London SW1X 8QB (tel: 01-235 0831).
Educational Office: 29 Belgrave Square (tel: 01-245 6481).
Ministry of Education: Airport Road, Riyadh.

Saudi schools segregate the sexes from primary school to university. There are openings for male TEFL teachers, mainly in the private sector. There are Saudi Arabian International Schools at Al Khobar, Dhahran, Jeddah, Jubail and Riyadh. Other international schools catering for expatriates are: Aramco Schools (Dhahran); Continental School, Jeddah Preparatory School (Jeddah); International School (Yanbu).
   Foreign teachers are also used at the university level, and here there are a few opportunities for women. The country's universities are: King Abdul Aziz, Jeddah, with a branch at Taif; King Saud, Riyadh, with branches at Abha and Qaseem; King Feisal, Dammam and Hofuf, and University of Petroleum and Minerals, Dhahran.
   The British Council operates its own language institutes and there are a number of private sector language schools as well. Foreign companies are often required to run training programmes for their Saudi staff. ARAMCO and British Aerospace are the leaders in this respect, but Saudi Airlines and hospital management companies also run such programmes. Ministries, such as the Foreign Ministry, also need expatriate teachers, notably TEFL experts.
   Saudia Arabia is a very conservative Muslim society, where you must take care not to give offence. European women do not have to cover their faces now, but they are expected to cover everything else, and they are not allowed to drive cars. Alcohol is forbidden and opportunities to mix with the locals are very rare. Teachers are well paid, but most of the posts are bachelor status ones. Employers are responsible for obtaining work permits, etc. Among the documents you will probably have to produce a baptismal certificate and certification that you do not suffer from AIDS.
Recruitment: AMI; ARA; British Aerospace; British Council; ECIS.

SENEGAL   Pop: 6.4m   Area: 196,000 sq km   GNP: $380
Embassy: 11 Phillimore Gardens, London W8 7QG (tel: 01-937 0925).
Ministry of Education: BP 699, Dakar.

Education is based on the French system, but modified to cope with the country's present day needs. The Central Bureau recruits assistants for lycées and the British Senegalese Institutes. The American Cultural Centre and the Centre de Perfectionnement en Langue Anglaise also employ foreign TEFL teachers. International education is provided by two small establishments: the Dakar Academy (BP 3189) and the International School (c/o US Embassy). At the tertiary level there is the University of Dakar, a second university at St Louis, the Ecole Polytechnique at Thies and a Regional Management School for CEAO member states.
Recruitment: British Council; Central Bureau.

SEYCHELLES   Pop: 65,000   Area: 308 sq km   GNP: $2,430
High Commission: 2 Mill Street, London W1R 9TE.
Ministry of Education: PO Box 48, Mont Fleuri.

Education is based on the British comprehensive system. Crown Agents recruit around ten teachers a year for government schools. There is a small International School at Victoria (PO Box 315). The islands also boast a polytechnic, a technical college and a teacher training college.
Recruitment: Crown Agents; ODA.

SIERRA LEONE   Pop: 3.5m   Area: 72,000 sq km   GNP: $380
High Commission: 33 Portland Place, London W1N 3AG (tel: 01-636 6483).
Ministry of Education: New England, Freetown.

There are an AIS and an International School in Freetown, and the Kabala Rupp Memorial School in Kabala. There are also four teacher training colleges and a university — the University of Sierra Leone which has three constituent parts: Fourah Bay College, Njala University College and the Institute of Education.
Recruitment: ACU; VSO.

SINGAPORE   Pop: 2.6m   Area: 581 sq km   GNP: $7,260
High Commission: 2 Wilton Crescent, London SW1X 8RW (tel: 01-235 8315).
Ministry of Education: Kay Siang Road, Singapore 1024.

This prosperous island state is determined to improve educational standards, which are already high, especially in English teaching. The objective is to make English the medium of instruction in all schools. The High Commission recruits teachers for both the secondary and the tertiary level through its section at 5 Chesham Street, London SW1X 8ND (tel: 01-235 9067).

The international education sector is represented by the United World College of SE Asia, International School and the American School as well as some primary establishments. Tertiary level institutions include the National University of Singapore, Nanyang Technological Institute, Singapore Polytechnic, Ngee Ann Polytechnic, Institute of Education. *Recruitment:* ACU; High Commission; International House.

SOLOMON ISLANDS   Pop: 270,000   Area: 28,000 sq km
GNP: $680
Ministry of Education: PO Box 584, Honiara.

The islands boast a teachers' college, Honiara Technical Institute, and the Honiara Centre of the University of the Pacific.
Recruitment: ODA; VSO.

SOMALIA   Pop: 4.7m   Area: 637,000 sq km   GNP: $250
Embassy: 60 Portland Place, London W1N 3DG (tel: 01-580 7148).
Ministry of Education: Mogadishu.

Apart from the small American School in Mogadishu, all educational establishments are run by the state. Enrolments are low: 25% receive primary education; 8% attend secondary school. In addition, the Government runs ten training centres for nomads. At the tertiary level there are two teacher training colleges and the University of Mogadishu.
Recruitment: British Council; ECIS.

SOUTH AFRICA: Pop: 33m   Area: 1.2m sq km
GNP: $2,260
Embassy: South Africa House, Trafalgar Square, London WC2N 5DP
    (tel: 01-930 4488).
Department of National Education: Private Bag X122, Pretoria 0001.

South Africa is reckoned to have the highest educational standards in the whole of Africa for all races. However, expatriates are often hesitant to move here, because of distaste for the politics of the régime. Education is the responsibility of the provincial governments, and enquiries should be sent to the addresses below.
Cape of Good Hope: PO Box 13, Cape Town
Natal: Private Bag X9044, Pietermaritzburg
Transvaal: Private Bag X76, Pretoria
Orange Free State: PO Box 521, Bloemfontein
South West Africa — Namibia: Windhoek (Namibia is not a province

but a territory administered by South Africa, but this situation is expected to change soon).

Opportunities exist especially for specialists in science, maths, business and technical subjects at all levels of the educational system. There are American International Schools in Capetown and Johannesburg. People wishing to enter the teaching profession will need to have their qualifications evaluated by the Advisory Committee for the Training of Teachers (Private Bag X55, Pretoria). There are ten white universities, which are also attended by Africans, Asians and Coloureds. In addition, there are four African-only universities in South Africa proper, and another four in the tribal homelands of Bophuthatswana, Ciskei, Transkei and Venda.

Recruitment: ECIS; Embassy.

SPAIN   Pop: 38.3m   Area: 505,000 sq km   GNP: $4,470
Embassy: 24 Belgrave Square, London SW1X 8QA (tel: 01-235 5555).
Consular Section: 20 Draycott Place, London SW3 (tel: 01-581 5921).
Spanish Institute: 102 Eaton Square, London SW1 (tel: 01-235 1485).
Consulates also in Liverpool (21 Rodney Street, L1 9EF) and
    Manchester (70 Spring Gardens, M2 2BQ).
Ministry of Education: Alcalá 34, Madrid 14.

Opportunities in state secondary schools tend to be restricted to exchange assistantships. However, the range of international schools is extensive. Such schools exist in Alicante, Barcelona (six), Bilbao, Cadiz, the Canary Islands (three), Ibiza (one), Madrid (eleven), Mallorca (five), Marbella (two), Sotogrande, Torremolinos and Valencia (two). The National Association of British Schools, Runnymede College, Arga 9, 1 Piso, Madrid 2 can provide further information. There are unlimited opportunities for TEFL teachers in Spain. The British Council has its own language institutes in Madrid, Barcelona, Valencia and Granada, and there are a number of institutes affiliated to English language teaching organisations. The British Institute, Almagro 5, Madrid 28010 produces a list of these. Other opportunities exist in the tertiary sector.

Generally speaking, if you are intending to work more than three months in Spain it is advisable for your employer to obtain a work permit in advance. When Spain achieves full EC membership, EC nationals will be able to work for three months without such a permit, but currently there is a good deal of red tape to contend with.

Recruitment: British Council; Central Bureau; ELT; Inlingua; International House.

SRI LANKA   Pop: 16m ·   Area: 65,600 sq km   GNP: $361
High Commission: 13 Hyde Park Gardens, London W2 2LX (tel:
01-262 1841).
Ministry of Education: 255 Banddhaloka Mawatha, Colombo 7.
Ministry of Higher Education: 18 Ward Place, Colombo 7.

There are two international schools in Sri Lanka: Colombo International School and the Overseas Children's School in Battarmulla. Sri Lanka has seven universities: Colombo, Peradinya, Jaffna, Sri Jayaawardenepura, Morutawa, Kelaniya and Ruhina. In addition there is an Open University and the University College of Baticaloa.
Recruitment: British Council; ECIS; VSO.

SUDAN   Pop: 21m   Area: 2.5m sq km   GNP: $340
Embassy: 3 Cleveland Row, London SW1A 1DD (tel: 01-839 8080).
Ministry of Education: Khartoum.

Sudan's education system, which was once one of the most advanced in Africa, has declined in recent years as a result of civil war, the withdrawal of British educators and the policy of Arabicisation introduced in the 1960s. The Government recognises the importance of English in the development of the country and in the mid-seventies introduced its own ELT scheme, for which the Embassy carries out recruitment. At any one time there are 200 ELT scheme teachers working throughout Sudan — usually in higher secondary schools (16-19). A full briefing is held at Farnham Castle in the summer, and teachers take up their posts in July and August. There is an American School in Khartoum.

The British Council recruits for posts in the Ministry of Education and in teacher training. There are universities at Khartoum, Juba, Gezira and Wadi Medani as well as a branch of the University of Cairo in Khartoum. Khartoum also has a Polytechnic.

English is the language of instruction in the south, and here a number of missionary agencies are active.
Recruitment: Sudanese Embassy; British Council; Volunteer Missionary Movement; VSO; Sudan United Mission (27 Granville Road, Sidcup DA14 4BU).

SURINAME   Pop: 390,000   Area: 163,000 sq km
GNP: $3,520
Ministry of Education: Sumnel Kaffiludistraat 117-123, Paramaribo.

Education in this South American state became compulsory between the ages of 6 and 12 back in 1878. It is a modified version of the Dutch

system. There may be teaching opportunities at the University of
Suriname in Paramaribo.

SWAZILAND   Pop: 700,000   Area: 17,000 sq km
GNP: $900
High Commission: 58 Pont Street, London SW1X 0AE (tel: 01-581
4976/7/8).
Ministry of Education: PO Box 39, Mbabane.

With an 85% enrolment at the primary level, Swaziland's educational
system is more impressive than those of many of its neighbours to the
north. There are opportunities in all subjects, including agriculture. The
capital, Mbabane, is home to the Waterford Kamhlaba United World
College of Southern Africa and the Sifundzani International School.
Tertiary level education is provided by the University of Swaziland,
Swaziland College of Technology and the Institute of Management and
Public Administration.
Recruitment: British Council; ECIS; ODA: IVS.

SWEDEN   Pop: 8.5m   Area: 459,000 sq km   GNP: $11,900
Embassy: 11 Montagu Place, London W1H 2AL (tel: 01-214 2101).
Ministry of Education: Mynttorget 1, 103 33 Stockholm.

As a rule, it is not possible for a non-Swede to work in a Swedish school
except under an exchange scheme. An exception is made in the case
of the British Centre as well as the English Centre in the South, both
of which provide TEFL teachers for the adult folk universities and
sometimes for secondary schools as well. For university posts it is best
to apply direct to the university concerned.
    International schools are, however, a different matter. Here are the
addresses of the main ones:
SSHL, IB-linjen, Box 8, S-193 00, Sigtuna
International School of Stockholm, Johannesgatan 18, S111 38
Stockholm
The British Primary School, Östra Valhallavägen 17, S-182 62
Djursholm
The English Junior School, Lilla danska vägen 1, S-412 74, Göteborg
    Sweden is not a member of the EC and it is necessary for everybody,
including EC nationals, to have a visa and work permit before they
arrive. It can take up to two months to obtain the necessary documen-
tation. You should make an appointment for an interview at the Em-
bassy and provide two photographs, a written offer of employment,
and your passport.
Recruitment: Central Bureau; International Language Services; The
English Centre, Stororget 8, 211 34 Malmö.

SWITZERLAND   Pop: 6.5m   Area: 41,300 sq km   GNP: $16,000
Embassy: 16-18 Montagu Place, London W1H 2BQ (tel: 01-723 0701).

Many are attracted to live and work in Switzerland, but few are chosen. State schools are the responsibility of each canton, and usually the only way into one is under an exchange scheme. The private school sector is normally overwhelmed with applications. The private schools have an association: Verband Schweizersicher Privatschulen, Zeughausgasse 29, Postfach 3367, 3000 Bern 7.

There are international schools and colleges galore: Basel (International); Berne (English International, International); Chateau d'Oex (Institut Alpin); Chesières-Villars (Aiglon College); Crans-Montana (International); Geneva (Collège de Léman, International, English); Gstaad (John F. Kennedy); Hasliberg-Goldern (Ecole d'Humanité); Lausanne (Commonwealth-American, Brillantmont, Ecole Nouvelle, Inst. Dr Schmidt, Château Mont-Choisi, Le Rosey); Leysin (American); Lugano (American); Montreux (Château Beau-Cèdre, Inst. Mont Rosa, St George's); Neuchâtel (Junior, Inst. auf dem Rosenberg); Zug (American); Zürich (AIS, Inter-Community, International Primary).

The restrictive immigration policy of the Swiss Government has made it difficult for foreigners to obtain residence permits with a view to taking up employment. The employer has to apply for a work permit to the Cantonal Aliens Police which issues an Assurance of Residence Permit. This must be shown to the immigration authorities on arrival in Switzerland. You must register with the police within eight days and undergo a medical examination.
Recruitment: Central Bureau; British Council; ECIS.

SYRIA   Pop: 11m   Area: 185,000 sq km   GNP: $2,000
Diplomatic Representation: 8 Belgrave Square, London SW1 8PH (tel: 01-245 9012).
Ministry of Education: Damascus.

There are two international schools of note: the Community School in Damascus and the ICARDA International School in Aleppo which serves the children of expatriates working at this research centre. The British Council has a language institute at Damascus, and there are some 25 schools offering evening classes in English. There are universities at Aleppo, Damascus and Lataki, and also the Homs School of Petroleum.
Recruitment: British Council; ECIS.

TAIWAN   Pop: 19.3m   Area: 36,000 sq km   GNP: $3,144
Representation: The Free Chinese Centre, 4th Floor, Dorland House,
    14-16 Regent Street, London SW1Y 4PH (tel: 01-930 5767).
Ministry of Education: 5 Chungshan Road, Taipei 100.

This dynamic island offers opportunities for foreign teachers especial-
ly at its international schools at Hsinchu (International), Taichung
(Morrison Academy), and Taipei (Dominican Academy, American
School). Taiwan has several private language schools and some 28 ter-
tiary institutions, notably the National Taiwan University, 1 Roosevelt
Rd IV, Taipei.

TANZANIA   Pop: 22m   Area: 945,000 sq km   GNP: $210
High Commission: 43 Hertford Street, London W1Y 7TF (tel: 01-499
    8951).
Ministry of Education: PO Box 9121, Dar es Salaam.

Since independence Tanzania has striven hard to adapt its educational
system to suit local conditions with mixed success. Around 61% at-
tend primary school, and the numbers in secondary schools are increas-
ing. There are a number of international schools: Arusha International,
Arusha; International, Dar es Salaam; Canon Andrea Mwaka,
Dodoma; Morogoro International Primary School; International
School, Moshi; Victoria Primary School, Mwanza. At the tertiary level
there may be opportunities at the University of Dar es Salaam, Sokoine
University of Agriculture or the two technical colleges.
Recruitment: British Council; ECIS; VSO.

THAILAND   Pop: 53m   Area: 514,000 sq km   GNP: $850
Embassy: 30 Queen's Gate, London SW7 5JB (tel: 01-589 0173).
Ministry of Education: Rajdamnern Avenue, Bangkok.

Generally speaking, Thailand is self-sufficient in teachers and lecturers,
where the medium of instruction is Thai. However, opportunities exist
for TEFL specialists in secondary education (volunteers), and for contract teachers at the tertiary level and in language institutes. International education is provided along British lines by the Bangkok
Patana School and the Traill Preparatory School. There are two other
international schools in Bangkok (International, Ruam Rudee) and one
in Chiengmai (Chiengmai International). At the tertiary level opportunities sometimes occur at universities, such as Chulalongkorn, Medical
Science, Fine Arts, Ramkhamhaeng, Kasetsart and Thammasart in
Bangkok; Chiengmai, Khonkhaen and Songkhla in the provinces. The
international Asian Institute of Technology north of Bangkok has a
substantial expatriate staff.

Recruitment: British Council; ECIS; VSO.

TOGO   Pop: 3m   Area 57,000 sq km   GNP: $280
Embassy: 30 Sloane Street, London SW1 (tel: 01-235 0147)
Ministry of Education: Immeuble des Quatre Ministères, rue Colonel
   de Roux, Lomé.

Togo was originally a German colony and was held up as a model.
Nowadays the country can boast that around 75% of the population
receives a primary education, one of the highest rates in West Africa.
Half of the schools are mission establishments. Self-help is encouraged
and local communities often build their own primary schools. The
World Bank has helped establish two teacher training colleges and the
National Institute of Agricultural Training. Tertiary education is provided by the University of Lomé and the University of Bénin at Lomé,
where there are TEFL opportunities. There is a tiny American school
in the capital.
Recruitment: British Council.

TONGA   Pop: 104,000   Area: 700 sq km   GNP: $740
High Commission: New Zealand House, Haymarket, London SW1X
   4TE (tel: 01-837 3287).
Ministry of Education: Nukualofa, Tonga.

There are around 50 foreign teachers in these South Pacific islands at
all levels, with science, maths, technical and business subjects being
most in demand.
Recruitment: VSO.

TRINIDAD & TOBAGO   Pop: 1.2m   Area: 5,000 sq km
GNP: $7,140
High Commission: 42 Belgrave Square, London SW1X 8NT (tel: 01-242
   9351).
Ministry of Education: Hayes Street, Port of Spain.

A prosperous republic with a well developed educational system. St
Andrew's School and Bishop Anstey Junior School, both in Port of
Spain, offer an international curriculum. Tertiary institutions include
the East Caribbean Farm Institute, the Polytechnic Institute and the
Trinidad campus of the UWI at St Augustine.
Recruitment: ACU; League for the Exchange of Commonwealth
Teachers.

TUNISIA   Pop: 7m   Area: 164,000 sq km   GNP: $1,280
Embassy: 29 Prince's Gate, London SW7 1QG (tel: 01-584 8117).
Ministry of Education: Place de la Kasbah, Tunis.

As a consequence of a strong interest in learning English in this former
French North African colony a Lycée Pilote has been set up by the
Ministry of Education, in which science subjects are taught through
the medium of English. An assistantship exchange scheme is in opera-
tion at the secondary level, and other opportunities in TEFL may oc-
cur at the University of Tunis, notably the Institut Bourguiba des
Langues Vivantes. There is a small American Co-operative School in
Tunis with an international clientele.
Recruitment: British Council; Central Bureau.

TURKEY   Pop: 50m   Area: 780,000 sq km   GNP: $1,200
Embassy: 43 Belgrave Square, London SW1X 8PA (tel: 01-235 0360).
Consulate: Rutland Lodge, Rutland Gardens, London SW7 (tel: 01-589
0360).
Ministry of Education: Ankara.

In the past five years there has been a boom in English teaching in
Turkey at all levels, especially in Istanbul, Izmir and Ankara, because
of the trend towards bilingual 'Anatolian' schools (using both Turkish
and English as the medium of instruction) and English medium courses
at universities. A large number of private 'Anatolian' schools have been
set up to cope with demand, while other established private schools
have gone over to the 'Anatolian' system, which involves one year on
intensive English. Science and maths teachers are also required.
    The state universities employ a sizeable number of foreign teachers,
mostly in TEFL, and demand may increase as private universities, currently at the planning stage, come into being.
    A number of private language schools are flourishing in the main
centres, but the schools run by the ITBA in Istanbul and the IBA in
Ankara are the most prestigious. These are independent foundations
with British Council links. The British Council in Istanbul keeps a list
of language schools and 'Anatolian' schools in Western Turkey, and
its counterpart in Ankara has information for the rest of the country.
Several institutions advertise for staff in the *Times Educational
Supplement.*
    The recruitment process can be a lengthy one, especially in the case
of private schools, as Ministry approval has to be obtained. The
preference is for teachers with degrees in English, but the regulations
are apt to change.
Recruitment: Anchor; British Council; Christians Abroad; ELT;
International House.

TUVALU   Pop: 8,000   Area: 25 sq km   GNP: $680
Ministry of Education: Vaiaku, Funafati.

Formerly the Ellice Islands, Tuvalu's primary and secondary institutions have recently been joined by a centre of the University of the South Pacific at Funafati.
Recruitment: ODA; VSO.

UGANDA   Pop: 13m   Area: 236,000 sq km   GNP: $230
High Commission: Uganda House, Trafalgar Square, London WC2N 5DX (tel: 01-839 5783).
Ministry of Education: Kampala

Life is slowly returning to normal in this scenically-attractive country after years of bloodshed. Uganda faces a severe shortage of teachers in most subjects. Many of the secondary schools are private or semi-private. The Lincoln International School functions in Kampala. The country boasts the oldest tertiary foundation in East Africa — Makerere University.
Recruitment: BCMS; Rwanda Mission; VSO.

USSR   Pop: 278m   Area: 22.5m sq km   GNP: $4,550
Embassy: 13 Kensington Palace Gardens, London W8 4QX (tel: 01-229 6412).
Ministry of Education: Shabolovka Ul. 33, Moscow.
Ministry of Higher Education & Secondary Specialised Education: Lyusinovskaya Ul. 51, Moscow.

Opportunities are minimal and recruitment, normally to university posts, is done at an official level, except in the case of the Anglo-American school in Moscow. Now that we are in the era of *glasnost,* perhaps more opportunities will occur in the future .
Recruitment: British Council; ECIS.

UNITED ARAB EMIRATES   Pop: 1.6m   Area: 83,600 sq km GNP: $22,000
Embassy: 30 Prince's Gate, London SW7 1PT (tel: 01-581 1281).
Ministry of Education: PO Box 295, Abu Dhabi.

Formerly the Trucial States, this is a federation of seven Arab states, each proud of its own traditions. The largest are Abu Dhabi and Dubai. UAE nationals form only a minority of the population. There is a large continent of expatriate teachers mainly from other Arab countries, teaching in the state system. There are opportunities for Europeans at the University of Al Ain and at the training centre of the state oil company ADMA-OPCO.

The British Council has its own language institutes in Abu Dhabi and Dubai, and there are private ventures, such as the Polyglot School in Dubai and the Al Bayyan Institute, Sharjah. There are a number of international schools and English medium schools employing foreign teachers. Abu Dhabi (Al Rabbeh School, Alkubairat School, American Community School, International School of Choueifat); Al Ain (English Speaking School, International School); Dubai (Cambridge High School, Dubai College, English Speaking School, Jebel Ali School, Jumairah American School, Jumairah English Speaking School, Rashid School for Boys); Ras El Kahimah (English Speaking School); Sharjah (Al Qasinia Private School, International School, English School).
Recruitment: British Council; ECIS.

UNITED STATES OF AMERICA   Pop: 237m   Area: 9m sq km
GNP: $15,490
Embassy: Grosvenor Square, London W1A 1AE (tel: 01-499 9000). Consulates in Edinburgh and Belfast.

The US is more than self-sufficient in secondary school teachers, except in maths and science. The situation is slightly more promising in primary schools, particularly in the areas of bilingual education and special education.

Public education is the responsibility of each individual state, and their certification requirements can differ considerably from one state to another. Some may require teachers to be American citizens while others may require prospective teachers to have received a job offer from a state school before they can apply for certification. Private and parochial schools, however, are not usually bound by the requirements laid down by the state education authorities.

There are three courses of action you can take:
● apply to the appropriate State Board of Education, Division of Teacher Certification, to check the status of your qualifications and enquire about vacancies;
● write to the local Superintendent of Schools of the city or district where you would like to teach to enquire about vacancies;
● apply direct to the principals of private or parochial schools.
Appointments are usually made between Christmas and the spring.

There are a few international schools which prepare for British examinations and the International Baccalaureate. Among them are:
The Anglo-American School, 18 W 89th Street, New York, NY 10024
United Nations International School, 24-50 East River Drive, New York, NY 10010

Washington International School, 2735 Olive Street, Washington, DC
   20007
Dwight School, 402 E 67th St, New York, NY 10021.

   Teacher exchanges are handled by the Central Bureau and the British
American Exchange Foundation, 34 Belgrave Road, Seaford, E. Sussex.
If you wish to work permanently in the USA you will need to apply
for an immigrant visa, the processing of which can take up to nine
months. A useful source of information and addresses is the US/UK
Educational Commission, 6 Porter Street, London W1 (near Baker
Street Underground Station).
Recruitment: Central Bureau; ECIS.

URUGUAY   Pop: 3m   Area: 176,000 sq km   GNP: $2,000
Embassy: 48 Lennox Gardens, London SW1X 0DL (tel: 01-589 8835).
Ministry of Education: Sarandí 440, Montevideo.

This small compact country, with scenery reminiscent of the Cotswolds,
boasts only one sizeable city — Montevideo. There are a number of
international schools, notably the Crandon Institute, the American
School, St Catherine's and St Andrew's. The Anglo-Uruguayan Cultural
Institute has 25 regional branches teaching English and the American-
supported Alianza Cultural Uruguay-USA has 30. There are four tertiary institutions, including the Universidad de la República.
Recruitment: British Council.

VANUATU   Pop: 128,000   Area: 14,800 sq km   GNP: $350
Ministry of Education: PO Box 153, Port Vila.

Formerly the Anglo-French condominium of the New Hebrides, both
French and English are used as the medium of instruction. There are
ten secondary schools on the islands, together with a technical college
and a teacher training college. Plans are afoot to build a centre for the
University of the South Pacific at Port Vila.
Recruitment: ODA; VSO.

VENEZUELA   Pop: 17m   Area: 912,000 sq km
GNP: $3,220
Embassy: 1 Cromwell Road, London SW7 2HW (tel: 01-581 2776).
Ministry of Education: Edif Educación, esq El Conde, Caracas.

This oil-producing country operates a teacher exchange programme with
the UK. International schools include: Caracas (AIS, British School,
Escuela Campo Alegre, Leap); Maracaibo (Escuela Bella Vista); Valencia (Colegio International).

The British Council has its own language institutes in Caracas, Ciudad Guyana and Maracaibo; the US has two Bi-national Centres, and there are private language schools as well. Venezuela has over 20 state and private universities, and in order to overcome the shortage of skilled labour the Government have set up INCE, a national training institute. *Recruitment:* British Council; Central Bureau.

VIETNAM   Pop: 58m   Area: 333,000 sq km   GNP: $160
Embassy: 12 Victoria Road, London W8 5RD (tel: 01-937 1912).
Ministry of Education: 21 Le Thanh Tong, Hanoi.

The Vietnamese economy is in a depressed state and the country relies largely on aid from the Soviet bloc. There are opportunities for TEFL teachers in the 90 or so colleges of higher education and universities, but on a volunteer basis only.

YEMEN ARAB REPUBLIC (NORTH YEMEN)   Pop: 7m
Area: 195,000 sq km   GNP: $510
Embassy: 41 South Street, London W1Y 5PD (tel: 01-629 9905).
Ministry of Education: Sana'a.

The country is making a considerable effort to develop its educational system with help from its rich Arab neighbours. With the highest adult illiteracy rate in Asia (86.3%) it has a tremendous task on its hands. However, enrolment in primary schools now stands at 65%. Opportunities exist in the Sana'a International School, the bilingual Mohammed Ali Othman School in Taiz and the University of Sana'a. *Recruitment:* British Council.

YEMEN PEOPLE'S DEMOCRATIC REPUBLIC (SOUTH YEMEN)
Pop: 2m   Area: 333,000 sq km   GNP: $560
Embassy: 57 Cromwell Road, London SW7 2ED (tel: 01-584 6607).
Ministry of Education: Aden.

The Eastern bloc countries provide the country with much of its technical assistance. If there are opportunities for Westerners they are most likely to occur at the University of Aden, the agricultural school or one of the ten teacher training colleges.

YUGOSLAVIA   Pop: 23m   Area: 255,804 sq km
Embassy: 5 Lexham Gardens, London W8 5JJ (tel: 01-370 6105).

Education is the responsibility of the six individual republics and two autonomous provinces. The international School of Belgrade and the very small American School of Zagreb are the only international estab-

lishments. TEFL lecturers in Yugoslav universities, high schools and language centres are recruited through official channels.
Recruitment: British Council; ECIS.

ZAÏRE   Pop: 31m   Area: 2.3m sq km   GNP: $140
Embassy: 26 Chesham Place, London SW1X 8HH (tel: 01-235 6137).
Ministry of Primary & Secondary Education: Avenue des Ambassadeurs, BP 3/63, Kinshasa/Gombe.
Ministry of Higher Education: Avenue Colonel Tshatshi, Kinshasa/ Gombe.

Formerly the Belgian Congo. Belgian influence is still strong, and French is the official language of Zaïre. School teachers are expected to have a good working knowledge of French, except in the two international schools — the American School (BP 4702) and the Zaire British Association School (BP 940), both in Kinshasa. There is expatriate TEFL involvement at the English Language Centre, Kinshasa and the Institut National de Science et de l'Education.
Recruitment: British Council; Africa Inland Mission; Regions Beyond Missionary Union.

ZAMBIA   Pop: 7m   Area: 753,000 sq km   GNP: $470
High Commission: 2 Palace Gate, London W8 5NG (tel: 01-589 6655).
Ministry of General Education: PO Box RW 50093, Lusaka.
Ministry of Higher Education: PO Box 50464, Lusaka.

Zambia has more or less achieved its aim of universal primary education, and the next objective is to completely Zambianise the teaching corps. At the moment there is still expatriate involvement in schools. Opportunities exist at Kitwe (Lechwe School), Lusaka (International School), and Ndola (Nsansa School). There may be training opportunities with the mining companies of the Copper Belt as well as opportunities for lecturers at the University of Zambia or the fourteen teacher training colleges.
Recruitment: British Council; ECIS; VSO.

ZIMBABWE   Pop: 8m   Area: 390,500 sq km   GNP: $740
High Commission: 429 Strand, London WC2R 0SA (tel: 01-836 7755).
Ministry of Education: PO Box 8022, Causeway, Harare.

There are a number of opportunities for expatriates, but they tend now to be offered on contract rather than permanent terms. Education is non-racial at all levels, and virtually universal. Around 90% of children attend primary school. Among the leading private schools are Falcon

College at Esigodini, Arundel School in Harare and Peterhouse at Marondera. At the tertiary level expatriates are employed at the University of Zimbabwe, Harare Polytechnic and Bulawayo Technical College.
Recruitment: ACU; British Council; Christians Abroad; CIIR; Volunteer Missionary Movement; VSO.

LATE ENTRIES

LIBERIA   Pop: 2.2m   Area: 111,000 sq km   GNP: $500
Embassy: 2 Pembridge Place, London W2 4XB (tel: 01-221 1036).
Ministry of Education: PO Box 1545, Monrovia.

Educational provision is extensive: 75% of children attend primary school. Opportunities exist in the private sector and at international schools, the American Cooperative School and the British Preparatory School in Monrovia. Science, maths and technical specialists are needed, particularly at the tertiary level, which includes a college of technology, a computer science institute, Cuttington Episcopalean University College and the University of Monrovia.
Recruitment: VSO.

LIBYA   Pop: 3m   Area: 1.76m sq km   GDP: $8,230
No representation (Saudia Arabian Embassy looks after Libyan interests).
Secretariat of the General People's Committee for Education: Tripoli.

British expatriates work as instructors with oil companies and as teachers in the secondary and tertiary sectors. The oil companies run two international schools: the English Community School at Marsa Brega (Sirte Oil Co) and the Oil Companies School, PO Box 860, Tripoli. The three universities are: El Fateh in Tripoli, Ghar Yunis in Benghazi, and Marsa Brega.
Recruitment: Umm Al-Jawaby Oil Service Co Ltd, 33 Cavendish Square, London W1M 9HF.

LUXEMBOURG   Pop: 370,000   Area: 2,600 sq km   GDP: $13,650
Embassy: 27 Wilton Crescent, London SW1X 8SD (tel: 01-235 6961).
Ministry of Education: 6 bld Royal, L-2449 Luxembourg.

The education system is an amalgamation of French and German curricula. The Centre Universitaire has a multinational staff (162a ave de la Faiencerie). There is also an Institut Supérieur de Téchnologie, an Institut Supérieur d'Etudes Pédagogiques, and the European Institute for Information Management. There are two international schools: Ecole Européeane, Plateau de Kirchberg; the American School, 188 ave de la Faiencerie, and a number of private language schools.
Recruitment: DES: ECIS.

TABLE 1
AGENCIES WHICH RECRUIT FOR EDUCATIONAL POSITIONS ABROAD

Agency	Areas	Institutions	TEFL	Other	Number	Contract	Method
Anchor Language Services A	Turkey	I	X	-	40*	N1	AR
ARA Int'l A	MA	HC	X	T	20	N12	A
Assoc Commonwealth Univ A§	ASFCO	H	X	AMSTBD	1,300	N23U	A
AMI Mid East Services AE	Saudi	PC	X	MSTD	5	N12	AZ
Baptism MS A	AS	PS	X	MS	10	M3	
Bell Educ Trust AE	EMASFO	HIC	X	MST	20+	NU	A
British Aerospace E	M	C	X	T	variable	N1	A
British Council AE§	EMASF	HSIET	X	MST	250+	N123	A
Canning School E	Japan,Italy	I	X	B	7+	NU	A
Central Bureau (Teacher) A§	EN	S	X	AMS	150	X½1	AR
Central Bureau (Assistant) A§	EAL	SH	X	-	500	X1	AR
CBT E§	EMS	SHC	X	AMSTB	100+	N2	AZ
Christians Abroad A§	EAC	PSI	X	AMSTB	50	N12	A
Church of Scotland AE	AMSFLC	PSIT	X	AMST	6	M4	AZ
Crown Agents A	MA	S	-	MST	10	N2	A
DES A§	E	PS	-	AMST	5	→	A
ELT International	EMS	SI	X	-	40	N1	AR
ECIS A§	EMASFNL	PS	X	AMSTB	500	N23	ARZ
Gabbitas Truman & Thring A§	EMASFL	PSC	X	AMSTB	-	N123	AR
ILC Recruitment AE	EMSF	SHIC	X	-	many	N½123	AR
Inlingua AE§	EF	I	X	-	150	N1	AR
International House AE§	EMASFL	I	X	B	200+	N½12U	AR
Int'l Language Services AE	EF	IC	X	-	60	N123U	AR
IVS A§	A	HCT	X	MSTBE	15	V2	A
Japan Recruitment A	Japan	PSHIC	X	B	10*	N1	A
Language School Appts AE	EMS	PSIT	X	ABMT	80*	N12	ARZ
League C'wealth T A§	ASNCO	S	-	AMST	250+	X½1	
Linguarama E	EF	I	X	-	-	N½12	!
MSL International A	MASF	IC	X	MST	10	N	A
O'Grady Peyton	EMAFN	PHSIETC	X	AMSTB	250	N12	AR
ODA AE§	ASFO	SHT	X	MSTFB		N2	AR
PACES A	MS	PSC	X	AMST	100+	N12	AR
Queen's Eng Lang SchE	Japan	I	X	—	10	N1	A
Service Children's E§	EF	PS	-	AMST	300	N3	AR
SLS	EMA	C	X	-	50	N½	ARZ
VMM E	AO	SCT	X	MSBF	!	V2	A
VSO A§	ASFC	SHT	X	MSTE	500	V2	A
World Educ Services A	MAF	PS	X	AMB	30*	N	AR

KEY

Agency:
A = Acts as a recruitment agency
E = Recruits for own organisation
X = Teacher exchange organisation

Areas:
E = Europe; M = Middle East (including North Africa);
A = Africa; S = South & South East Asia; F = Far East &
Pacific; N = North America; C = Caribbean; L = Latin
America; O = Australasia & other areas

Institutions:
P = Primary Schools; S = Secondary & Middle
(Intermediate) Schools; H = Higher (Tertiary) Education;
I = Language Institutes; C = In-company training/Adult
Education; T = Technical Institutes

Other subjects:
A = Arts subjects; B = Business; M = Maths;
S = Science; F = Agriculture; T = Technical subjects;
D = Medicine; E = Teacher training

Contract:
N = Normal conditions apply; X = Exchange scheme;
M = Missionary Terms; V = Volunteer status
½ = less than 1 year; 1 = 1 year; 2 = 2 years, etc.
U = open-ended contract

Method of Recruitment:
A = Advertisement   R = Register/Database
Z = Recommendation

§   For a description of these agencies refer to Chapter 3
*   Number likely to rise
↑   Recruits from participants on teacher training courses
!   Unlimited demand
→   Initial probationary year followed by two further
      contracts of four years each

Useful Addresses

ORGANISATIONS WHICH RECRUIT TEACHERS & LECTURERS
(Asterisked organisations are included in the Table on p.158)

Africa Evangelical Fellowship, 30 Lingfield Road, London SW19 4PU.

Africa Inland Mission, 2 Vorley Road, London N19 5HE.

Airwork Ltd, Hurn Airport, Christchurch, Dorset BH23 6EB.

AMI Middle East Services*, 7/9 St James's Street, London SW1A 1EE.

Anchor Language Services*, 30 Brick Row Cottages, Babraham, Cambridge CB2 4AJ (0223-836017).

ARA International*, 17-19 Maddox Street, London W1R 0EY.

Association of Commonwealth Universities*, John Foster House, 36 Gordon Square, London WC1H 0PF (01-387 8572).

Baptist Missionary Society*, 93/97 Gloucester Place, London W1H 4AA.

Bell Educational Trust*, The Lodge, Red Cross Lane, Cambridge CB2 2QX.

Bible Churchmen's Missionary Society, 93 Gloucester Place, 251 Lewisham Way, London SE4 1XF.

British Aerospace*, Saudi Arabian Support Department, Warton Aerodrome, Preston, Lancs PR4 1LA.

British Council, Overseas Appointments Department, 65 Davies Street, London W1Y 2AA (01-499 8011).

Camphill Village Trust, Delrow House, Hillfield Lane, Aldenham, Watford WD2 8DJ.

Canning School*, 4 Abingdon Road, London W8 6AF (01-938 2111).

Catholic Institute for International Relations, 22 Coleman Fields, London N1 7AF.

Central Bureau for Educational Visits & Exchanges*, Seymour Mews House, Seymour Mews, London W1H 9PE (01-486 5101); 3 Brunstfield Crescent, Edinburgh EH10 4HD (031-447 8024); 16 Malone Road, Belfast BT9 5BN (0232-664418).

Centre for British Teachers*, Quality House, Quality Court, Chancery Lane, London WC2 (01-242 2982).

Christians Abroad*, 11 Carteret Street, London SW1H 9DL (01-222 2165).

Church of Scotland Board of World Mission and Unity*, 121 George Street, Edinburgh EH2 4YN.

Commonwealth Fund for Technical Co-operation, Marlborough House, Pall Mall, London SW1Y 5HX.

Council for World Mission, 25 Marylebone Road, London NW1 5JR.

Crown Agents*, St Nicholas House, St Nicholas Road, Sutton, Surrey SM1 1EL (01-643 3311).

Department of Education and Science (Schools Branch I)*, Elizabeth House, York Road, London SE1 7PH (01-934 9156).

ELT International*, 20 Horsefair, Banbury, Oxon OX16 0AH (0295-3480).

European Council of International Schools*, 18 Lavant Street, Petersfield, Hants GU32 3EW (0730-68244).

Exodus, 128 Balfron Tower, St Leonards Road, London E14 0RT.

Gabbitas, Truman & Thring*, Broughton House, 6-8 Sackville Street, London W1X 2BR (01-439 2071).

ILC Recruitment*, 1 Riding House Street, London W1A 3AS (01-580 4351).

Inlingua Teacher Service*, 28 Rotton Park Road, Birmingham B16 9JJ (021-455 6465).

International House, Teacher Selection Department*, 106 Piccadilly, London W1V 9FL (01-491 2598).

International Language Services*, 14 Rollerstone Street, Salisbury, Wilts SP1 1ED.

International Voluntary Service*, 3 Belvoir Street, Leicester LE1 6SL (0533-541862).

Japan Recruitment*, 5 Sherwood Street, London W1 (01-734 4421).

Kendall & Partners, 7 Albert Court, Prince Consort Road, London SW7 2BJ (01-589 1256).

Language School Appointments*, 27 Delancey Street, London NW1 7RX (01-388 6644).

League for the Exchange of Commonwealth Teachers*, Seymour Mews House, 26-37 Seymour Mews, London W1H 9PE (01-486 2849).

Linguarama*, 16 Waterloo Street, Birmingham B2 5UG.

Methodist Church Overseas Division, 25 Marylebone Road, London NW1 5JR.

MSL International*, Pilgrim House, 1/6 William Street, Windsor, Berks SL4 0BA (0753-842823).

O'Grady Peyton International*, 1 Glenthorne Road, London W6 0LF (01-708 9898); 37 Dawson Street, Dublin 2 (01-779 716).

Overseas Development Administration*, (Appointments Officer — Education), Abercrombie House, Eaglesham Road, East Kilbride G75 8EA (03552-41199).

PACES*, 6b Eccleston Gardens, St Helens WA10 3BN.

Papua New Guinea Church Partnership, 32 King's Orchard, Eltham, London SE9 5TJ.

Pitman Education and Training, 154 Southampton Row, London WC1B 5AX (01-580 8341).

Presbyterian Church in Ireland Overseas Board, Church House, Belfast BT1 6DW.

Queen's English Language Schools*, 51 New Park Street, Devizes, Wilts SN10 1DP; 3F Yuzuki Building, 4-7-14 Minimiyawata, Ichikawa 272, Japan.

Regions Beyond Missionary Union, 186 Kennington Park Road, London SE1 8UU.

Service Children's Education Authority*, Court Road, Eltham, London SE9 5NR.

South American Missionary Society, Allen Gardiner House, Pembury Road, Tunbridge Wells, Kent TN2 3QU.

Specialist Language Services*, Cromwell House, 13 Ogleforth, York YO1 2JG (0904-36771).

Sudan United Mission, 75 Granville Road, Sidcup DA14 4BU.

United Nations Association International Service, 3 Whitehall Court, London SW1A 2EL (01-930 0679).

Voluntary Service Overseas*, 9 Belgrave Square, London SW1X 8PW (01-235 5191).

Volunteer Missionary Movement*, Shenley Lane, London Colney, St Albans, Herts AL2 1AR (0727-24853).

Worldwide Education Service*, Strode House, 44-50 Osnaburgh Street, London NW1 3NN (01-387 9228).

Non-UK agencies

Anglo-American Teaching Service, Suite 23E, 100 W 92nd Street, New York, NY, USA.

Canadian University Service Overseas (CUSO), 135 Rideau Street, Ottawa, Canada.

ICM (Intergovernmental Committee for Migration: Geneva Office for Latin America), 17 route des Morillons, BP 100, 1211 Geneva 19, Switzerland.

International Schools Services, PO Box 5910, Princeton, NJ 08543, USA.

Overseas Schools Service, 446 Louise Street, Farmville, VA 23901, USA.

Overseas Service Bureau, PO Box 350, Fitzroy, 3065 Victoria, Australia.

SOURCES OF ADVICE & INFORMATION

Agency for Personal Service Overseas, 29 Fitzwilliam Square, Dublin 2.

British Council English Teaching Information Centre (ETIC), 10 Spring Gardens, London SW1A 2BN (01-930 8466).

Career Analysts, 90 Gloucester Place, London W1H 4BL (01-935 5452).

Career Assessment Services, Melbourne House, Melbourne Street, Brighton BN2 3LH (0273-675299).

Careers Advisory & Business Services, 18 Winchcombe Street, Cheltenham GL52 2LX (0242-2224616).

Centre for Information on Language Teaching & Research, Regent's College, Inner Circle, Regent's Park, London NW1 4NS (01-468 8221).

Centre for International Briefing, Farnham Castle, Surrey GU9 0AG (0252-721194).

Committee for International Co-operation in Higher Education, British Council, 10 Spring Gardens, London SW1A 2BN (01-930 8466).

Employment Conditions Abroad, Anchor House, 15 Britten Street, London SW3 3TY (01-351 7151).

Expatriate Briefings, Rectory Road, Great Waldingfield, Sudbury, Suffolk CO10 0TL (0787-78607).

Expats International, 62 Tritton Road, London SE21 8DE (01-670 8304).

Hospital for Tropical Diseases, 3 St Pancras Way, London NW1 0PE (01-387 4411).

Independent Assessment & Research Centre, 57 Marylebone High Street, London W1M 3AE (01-935 2373).
Independent Schools Information Service (ISIS), 56 Buckingham Gate, London SW1E 6AG (01-630 8793).

Liverpool School of Tropical Medicine, Pembroke Place, Liverpool L3 5QA (051-708 9393).
London University Institute of Education Library, 11-13 Ridgmount Street, London WC1 (01-637 0846).

Medical Advisory Services for Travellers Abroad Ltd (MASTA), Bureau of Hygiene & Tropical Diseases, Keppel Street, London WC1E 7HT (01-636 8636).
Mid-Career Development Centre, 77 Morland Road, Croydon CR0 6EA (01-654 0808).

Vocational Guidance Association, 7 Harley House, Upper Harley Street, London NW1 4RP (01-935 2600).

Women's Corona Society, Minster House, 274 Vauxhall Bridge Road, London SW1V 1BB (01-828 1652).

MISCELLANEOUS ADDRESSES

American International Schools, c/o US Embassy of the country in question.

Audio Forum, 31 Kensington Church Street, London W8 4LL (01-937 1647).

BBC Publications, 35 Marylebone High Street, London W1M 4AA.
Berlitz, 79 Wells Street, 321 Oxford Street, London W1A 3BZ.
British Airways Vaccination Unit, 75 Regent Street, London W1R 7HG (01-439 9584).

Department of Social Security, Overseas Branch, Newcastle-upon-Tyne NE98 1YX.

European Community Schools, see Department of Education & Science (Schools Branch I).

Inland Revenue Claims Branch, Foreign Division, Merton Road, Bootle L69 9BL.

International Baccalaureate Examinations Office, University of Bath, Claverton Down, Bath BA2 7AY (0225-62501).

International Baccalaureate European Office, 18 Woburn Square, London WC1H 0NS (01-637 1682).

International Educator's Institute, 25 Queen Anne's Gardens, Ealing, London W5 5QD; PO Box 103, West Bridgewater, MA 02379, USA.

Institution of Professional Civil Servants, see OCTAB.

Japan Exchange & Teaching Programme, c/o Gabbitas, Truman & Thring, 6-8 Sackville Street, London W1X 2BR.

Linguaphone, 124-126 Brompton Road, Kinghtsbridge, London SW3.

Overseas Contract Teachers & Advisers Branch (OCTAB), Institution of Professional Civil Servants, 75-79 York Road, London SE1 7AQ.

Regional Passport Offices:

Greater London: Clive House, 70 Petty France, London SW1H 9HD.

Midlands & Eastern England: 55 Westfield Road, Peterborough, PE3 6TG.

Northern England: 5th Floor, India Building, Water Street, Liverpool L2 0QZ.

Northern Ireland: Marlborough House, 30 Victoria Street, Belfast, BT1 3LY.

Scotland: 1st Floor, Empire House, 131 West Nile Street, Glasgow G1 2RY.

Wales & Western England: Olympia House, Upper Dock Street, Newport NP1 1XA.

Ross Institute, Bureau of Hygiene & Tropical Diseases, Keppel Street, London WC1E 7HT.

Thomas Cook, 45 Berkeley Square, London W1A 1EB (01-499 4000).

United Nations Volunteers, c/o 3 Whitehall Court, London SW1A 2EL.

United World Colleges, 1 Mecklenburgh Square, London W1.

Further Reading

Publishers' addresses are given at the end of the appendix.

CAREERS

Brits Abroad: A Guide to Living & Working in Developing Countries, Harry Brown & Rosemary Thomas (Express Books, 1981)

Changing Your Job After 35, Geoffrey Golzen & Philip Plumbley (Kogan Page, 1984)

The Directory of Jobs & Careers Abroad, David Leppard (Vacation Work Publications, 1989)

The Directory of Work & Study in Developing Countries, David Leppard (Vacation Work Publications, 1986)

How to Get a Job Abroad, Roger Jones (Northcote House, 1989)

How to Get That Job, Joan Fletcher (Northcote House, 1987)

How to Live & Work in America, Steve Mills (Northcote House, 1988)

How to Live & Work in Australia, Laura Veltman (Northcote House, 1987)

The International Directory of Voluntary Work (Vacation Work Publications, 1989)

What Can a Teacher Do Except Teach? Barbara Onslow (COIC, 1983)

Working Abroad, Geoffrey Golzen (Kogan Page, 1988)

Working Abroad? A Guide to the Fiscal & Financial Dos and Don'ts, Harry Brown (Northcote House, 1986)

Work Your Way Around the World, Susan Griffith (Vacation Work Publications, 1987)

Free booklets

Opportunities in Education Overseas, ODA

Teaching Overseas, British Council

Volunteer Work Abroad, Central Bureau for Educational Visits & Exchanges

COUNTRIES & REGIONS

Africa Guide (World of Information, annual)

Africa South of the Sahara (Europa, annual)

Asia & The Pacific (World of Information, annual)
British Expatriate Handbook: Africa (Directory Profiles, annual)
British Expatriate Handbook: Europe (Directory Profiles, annual)
British Expatriate Handbook: Far East (Directory Profiles, annual)
British Expatriate Handbook: Middle East (Directory Profiles, annual)
Business Travel Guide: Arabian Peninsula (Economist Publications, 1987)
Business Travel Guide: China (Economist Publications, 1988)
Business Travel Guide: France (Economist Publications, 1988)
Business Travel Guide: Germany (Economist Publications, 1988)
Business Travel Guide: Italy (Economist Publications, 1989)
Business Travel Guide: Japan (Economist Publications, 1987)
Business Travel Guide: South East Asia (Economist Publications, 1988)
Business Travel Guide: USA (Economist Publications, 1987)
Business Travel Guide: USSR (Economist Publications, 1989)
Business Traveller's Handbook: Africa (Michael Joseph, 1981)
Business Traveller's Handbook: Asia, Australasia & The South Pacific (Michael Joseph, 1981)
Business Traveller's Handbook: Central America, South America & The Caribbean (Michael Joseph, 1981)
Business Traveller's Handbook: Europe (Michael Joseph, 1981)
Business Traveller's Handbook: Middle East (Michael Joseph, 1981)
Business Traveller's Handbook: USA & Canada (Michael Joseph, 1982)
Far East & Australasia (Europa, annual)
Latin America & The Caribbean (World of Information, annual)
Middle East & North Africa (Europa, annual)
Middle East Review (World of Information, annual)
South America, Central America & The Caribbean (Europa, annual)
South American Handbook (Trade & Travel, annual)

EDUCATION

Adult Education in Developing Countries, E.K. Townsend Coles (Pergamon, 1969)
An African School: A Record of Experience, K. Elliot (Cambridge University Press, 1970)
Canadian Education in the 1980s, J. Donald Wilson (Detselig, Calgary, 1981)
Contemporary Chinese Education, Ed: Ruth Hayhoe (Croom Helm, 1984)
A Critical Analysis of School Science Teaching in Arab Countries, J.E. Arrayed (Longman, 1980)
The Development of Modern Education in the Gulf, S. Al-Misnad (Ithaca Press, London, 1985)

Developments in Technical & Vocational Education: A Comparative Survey (UNESCO, 1976)

Educating & Training Technicians, A. MacLennan (Commonwealth Secretariat, 1975)

The Educational System in the European Community, Ed: Lionel Elvin (NFER/Nelson, 1981)

Education & Development, Ed: R. Garrett (Croom Helm, 1984)

Education & Japan's Modernization, Makoto Aso & Ikuo Amano (Japan Times, 1983 — available at the Japanese Embassy)

Education & Schooling in America, G.L. Gutek (Prentice Hall, 1983)

Education & Society in Africa, Mark Bray, Peter B. Clarke & David Stephens (Edward Arnold, 1986)

Education & Society in the Muslim World, Ed: Mohammed Wasiullah Khan (Hodder & Stoughton, 1981)

Education, Culture & Politics in Modern France, W.D. Halls (Pergamon, 1976)

Education for a Changing Spain, John M. McNair (Manchester University Press, 1984)

Education in Africa: A Comparative Survey, A.B. Fafunwa & J.U. Aisuku (Allen & Unwin, 1982)

Education in Asia & The Pacific, R.R. Singh (UNESCO, PO Box 1425, Bangkok, 1986)

Education in Australia, Phillip E. Jones (David & Charles, 1974)

Education, Industrialisation & Technical Progress in Mexico, Jorge Padua (IIEP Paris, 1986)

Education in Korea: A Third World Success Story, J.E. Jayasuriya (Korean National Commission for UNESCO, 1983)

Education in Latin America, Eds: Colin Brock & Hugh Lawlor (Croom Helm, 1985)

Education in Latin America & The Caribbean: Trends & Prospects 1970-2000, J.B. Gimeno (UNESCO, 1983)

Education in Modern China, R.F. Price (Routledge & Kegan Paul, 1979)

Education in Modern Egypt: Ideals & Realities, G.D.M. Hyde (Routledge & Kegan Paul, 1978)

Education in Northern Nigeria, A. Ozigi & L. Ocho (Allen & Unwin, 1981)

Education in the Arab World, B.G. Massialas & S.A. Jarrar (Praeger, 1983)

Education in the Soviet Union, Mervyn Matthews (Allen & Unwin, 1982)

Education Policy & Development Strategy in the Third World, M.K. Bacchus (Avebury Gower Publishing Co, 1987)

Education, Race & Social Change in South Africa, J.A. Marcum (University of California Press, 1982)

Essays on Canadian Education, Nick Kach (Destelig, 1986)

Europe at School, Norman Newcome (Methuen, 1977)

International Handbook on Educational Systems, Eds: J. Cameron et al (John Wiley & Sons; Vol I, 1983; Vol II, 1983; Vol III, 1984)

An Introduction to Education in American Society, E.F. Provenzo Jnr (Charles E. Merrill, 1986)

Islam: Continuity & Change in the Modern World, John Obert Voll (Longman, 1982)

The Japanese School, Benjamin Duke (Praeger, 1986)

Jobs in Japan, John Wharton (Global Press, 1989)

Little England on the Veld, Peter Randall (Ravan Press, Johannesburg, 1982)

Making Science Laboratory Equipment: A Manual for Students & Teachers in Developing Countries, X.F. Carelse (John Wiley, 1983)

Other Schools & Ours, Edmund King (Holt Rinehart & Winston, 1979)

People Development in Developing Countries, Ross Matheson (Associated Business Programmes, 1978)

Rural Development: Putting the Last First, Robert Chambers (Longman, 1983)

Schooling in East Asia, Eds: R. Murray Thomas & T. Neville Postlethwaite (Pergamon, 1983)

Schooling in the Pacific Islands, R. Murray Thomas (Pergamon, 1984)

Schools in New Zealand Society, Eds: Graham H. Robinson & Brian T. O'Rourke (Longman Paul, 1980)

Secondary Education in Nigeria, S. Adesina & S. Ogunsagu (University of Ife Press, 1984)

Society, Schools & Progress in E. Europe, Nigel Grant (Pergamon, 1969)

Some Aspects of Education in Tanzania, E.A.K. Meena (Longman Tanzania, 1983)

Teacher Education in ASEAN, Ed: Frances Wong (Heinemann, 1976)

Teaching Tactics for Japan's English Classrooms, John Wharton (Global Press, 1989)

World Education Series (American Association of Collegiate Registrar & Admissions Officers — up-to-date reviews of education in individual countries)

GENERAL & REFERENCE

Commonwealth Universities Yearbook (Association of Commonwealth Universities, annual)

Commonwealth Yearbook (HMSO, annual)
Dictionary of Symptoms, Dr Joan Gomez (Paladin, 1975)
ECIS Directory (ECIS, annual)
Grants Register (Macmillan, 1988)
Learning Languages: Where & How: Le guide mondial des centres des langues (Wie & Wo Verlag, 1985)
Successful Expatriation: Bridging the Culture Gap, David Wheatley (Employment Conditions Abroad, 1989)
Travellers' Health, Dr Richard Dawood (Oxford University Press, 1989)
The Tropical Traveller, John Hatt (Pan, 1982)
The UNESCO Statistical Yearbook (UNESCO, annual)
Wives Abroad, Cecilia Leong Salobir (published by the author, 1988; available from the Castle Bookshop, Farnham Castle, see p.51)
Working Holidays (Central Bureau for Educational Visits & Exchanges, annual)
World of Learning (Europa, annual)

PERIODICALS

Comparative Education Review (Carfax Publishing Co, PO Box 25, Abingdon, Oxon OX14 3UE)
Edited by Dr Edmund J. King, this is a scholarly publication which appears three times a year. It includes articles on educational developments both at home and abroad and reviews of recent books.

EFL Gazette (Loop Format Ltd, 10 Wright's Lane, London W8 6TA tel: 01-938 1818)
Edited by Melanie Butler, this is a monthly newspaper for TEFL teachers both in the UK and abroad. Together with the *Times Educational Supplement* and the *Guardian* it is the main advertising medium for TEFL posts. The organisation also publishes the *Careers Handbook for English Language Teaching.*

The Expatriate (22 Brighton Road, South Croydon, Surrey CR2 6EA, tel: 01-681 5545)
A monthly newsletter with subscribers in 70 countries, dealing with all matters of concern to people working abroad, including country briefings and advice on health, finance and legal matters. It also includes regular listings of jobs abroad and a guide to comparative costs of living and housing around the world.

ExpatXtra (PO Box 300, Jersey, Channel Islands, tel: 0534-36241)
A monthly newspaper with readers in 160 countries with particular emphasis on financial and legal matters.

Home & Away (Expats International Ltd, 62 Tritton Road, London SE21 8DE, tel: 01-670 8304)
The monthly magazine of Expats International, an organisation with 8,000 members, dealing with all matters of concern to expatriates, including finance, family matters and overseas jobs markets. Subscribers, who are generally on overseas contracts, also receive an extensive list of vacancies in the UK and abroad, and can have their details circulated to employers registered with the organisation.

Inside Tracks (Christopher Woodley, 10 Hartswood Road, London W12 2GQ)
A monthly publication which includes country reports.

Jobfinder (Overseas Consultants, PO Box 152, Isle of Man)
A fortnightly jobs bulletin which includes some teaching vacancies.

Resident Abroad (Editorial: Financial Times Business Information, 102-108 Clerkenwell Road, London EC1M 5SA, tel: 01-251 9321; subscriptions: Central House, 17 Park Street, Croydon CR0 1YD, tel: 01-680 3786)
A magazine concentrating on expatriate financial matters and carrying extensive financial advertising and analysis.

TIE (The International Educator's Institute, PO Box 103, West Bridgewater, MA 02379, USA)
A quarterly newspaper for teachers in international schools, the July issue of which is devoted entirely to vacancies.

Times Educational Supplement (Priory House, St John's Lane, London EC1M 4BX)
A weekly publication which includes educational news from other countries and an extensive overseas appointments section. The major agencies advertise here, and there are usually plenty of advertisements placed by overseas establishments, too.

Times Higher Education Supplement (Priory House, St John's Lane, London EC1M 4BX)
A weekly publication which concentrates on the tertiary sector of education. In each issue there are usually a number of advertisements for lecturing posts abroad, most of them in Commonwealth countries.

PUBLISHERS

George Allen & Unwin, Unwin Hyman Ltd, 15-17 Broadwick Street, London W1V 1FP

American Association of Collegiate Registrar & Admissions Officers, 1 Dupont Circle NW, Suite 330, Washington DC 20036, USA

Edward Arnold (Publishers) Ltd, 41 Bedford Square, London WC1B 3DQ

Associated Business Programmes, Ludgate House, 107-111 Fleet Street, London EC4A 2AB

Association of Commonwealth Universities, John Foster House, 26 Gordon Square, London WC1H 0PF

Avebury Gower Publishing Co, Gower House, Croft Road, Aldershot, Hants GU11 3HR

Cambridge University Press, The Edinburgh Building, Shaftesbury Road, Cambridge CB2 2RU

Central Bureau for Educational Visits & Exchanges, Seymour Mews House, Seymour Mews, London W1H 9PE

COIC, Sales Department, MSC, Moorfoot, Sheffield S1 4PQ

Commonwealth Secretariat, Marlborough House, Pall Mall, London SW1Y 5HX

Croom Helm Ltd, Provident House, Burrell Row, Beckenham, Kent BR3 1AT

David & Charles Ltd, Brunel House, Newton Abbot, Devon TQ12 4PU

Detselig, distributed by Lavis Marketing, 73 Lime Walk, Headington, Oxford OX3 7AD

Directory Profiles Ltd, 51A George Street, Richmond, Surrey TW9 1HJ

ECIS (European Council of International Schools), 18 Lavant Street, Petersfield, Hants GU32 3EW

Economist Publications Ltd, 40 Duke Street, London W1A 1DW

Employment Conditions Abroad, Anchor House, 15 Britten Street, London SW3 3TY

Europa Publications Ltd, 18 Bedford Square, London WC1B 3JN

Express Books, 121-128 Fleet Street, London EC4P 4JT

Global Press, distributed by Vacation Work Publications

William Heinemann Ltd, 10 Upper Grosvenor Street, London W1X 9PA

HMSO Books, St Crispins, Duke Street, Norwich NR3 1PD

Hodder & Stoughton Ltd, PO Box 700, Mill Road, Dunton Green, Sevenoaks, Kent TN13 2YA

Holt Rinehart & Winston, 33 The Avenue, Eastbourne, E. Sussex BN21 3UN

IIEP (International Institute for Education Planning), 7-9 rue Eugène Delacroix, 75116 Paris, France)

Ithaca Press, 13 Southwark Street, London SE1 1RQ

Michael Joseph Ltd, 27 Wrights Lane, London W8 5DZ

Kogan Page Ltd, 120 Pentonville Road, London N1 9JN

Longman Group UK Ltd, Longman House, Burnt Mill, Harlow, Essex CM20 2JE

Macmillan Ltd, 4 Little Essex Street, London WC2R 3LF

Manchester University Press, Oxford Road, Manchester M13 9PL

Charles E. Merrill Publishing International, Finsbury Business Centre, 40 Bowling Green Lane, London EC1R 0NE

Methuen & Co Ltd, 11 New Fetter Lane, London EC4P 4EE

Thomas Nelson & Sons Ltd, Nelson House, Mayfield Road, Walton-on-Thames, Surrey KT12 5PL

Northcote House Publishers Ltd, Harper & Row House, Estover Road, Plymouth, Devon PL6 7PZ

Oxford University Press, Walton Street, Oxford OX2 6DP

Paladin, 8 Grafton Street, London W1X 3LA

Pan Books Ltd, 18-21 Cavaye Place, London SW10 9PG

Pergamon Press, Headington Hill Hall, Oxford OX3 0BW

Praeger Publishers, 521 Fifth Avenue, New York, NY 10175, USA

Prentice-Hall International (UK) Ltd, 66 Wood Lane End, Hemel Hempstead, Herts HP2 4RG

Ravan Press, PO Box 31134, Berea, Johannesburg 2001, South Africa

Routledge & Kegan Paul Ltd, 11 Fetter Lane, London EC4P 1EE

Trade & Travel Publications, 5 Prince's Buildings, George Street, Bath

UNESCO, distributed by HMSO

University of California Press Ltd, 126 Buckingham Palace Road, London SW1W 9SD

University of Ife Press Ltd, Ile Ife, Nigeria

Vacation Work Publications, 9 Park End Street, Oxford OX1 1HJ

Wie & Wo Verlag, Am Hofgarten 5, Postfach 2464, D-5300 Bonn 1, West Germany

John Wiley & Sons Ltd, Baffins Lane, Chichester PO19 1UD

World of Information, 21 Gold Street, Saffron Walden, Essex CB10 1EJ

Index